TO THE POINT

EFFICIENT AND ATTRACTIVE WRITING
FOR ALMOST ANY AUDIENCE

D1706490

A.M. Tibbetts
University of Illinois at Urbana-Champaign

Scott, Foresman and Company
Glenview, Illinois

Dallas, Tex.   Oakland, N.J.   Palo Alto, Cal.
Tucker, Ga.   London, England

ACKNOWLEDGMENTS

Barnett. Lincoln Barnett, from *The Treasures of Our Tongue.* Copyright ©
1962, 1963, 1964 by Lincoln Barnett. Reprinted with permission of Lincoln
Barnett and Alfred A. Knopf. *Boyum.* "A Striking Spin Through Garp's
Weird World" by Joy Gould Boyum. Reprinted by permission of *The Wall
Street Journal,* July 23, 1982. Copyright © 1982 Dow Jones & Company, Inc.
All rights reserved. *Carter.* From "Crime Epidemic: 'It Can Happen to Me' "
by Hodding Carter III. Reprinted by permission of *The Wall Street Journal,*
January 14, 1982. Copyright © 1982 Dow Jones & Company, Inc. All rights
reserved. *Kronholz.* From "Shed No More Tears Over the Crocodile: It Has
Snapped Back" by June Kronholz. Reprinted by permission of *The Wall Street
Journal,* September 18, 1980. Copyright © 1980 Dow Jones & Company, Inc.
All rights reserved. *Mellinkoff.* David Mellinkoff, from *Legal Writing: Sense
and Nonsense.* Copyright © 1982 by David Mellinkoff. Reprinted with the per-
mission of Charles Scribner's Sons. *Morris.* From "Theodore Roosevelt,
President" by Edmund Morris from *American Heritage,* June/July 1981.
Copyright © 1981 by Edmund Morris. Reprinted by permission of Edmund
Morris and Georges Borchardt, Inc. *Steele.* A letter to American Honda
Company from Louise W. Steele, dated February 18, 1981. Reprinted by per-
mission of American Honda Company and Louise W. Steele. *Thomas.* From
"Getting a Grip on the Grippe" by Lewis Thomas from *Discover,* January
1982, vol. 3, p. 46. Copyright © 1981 Time Inc. Reprinted with
permission. *Wright.* Richard Wright, *Black Boy.* New York: Harper &
Brothers, 1937, p. 111.

Library of Congress Cataloging in Publication Data

Tibbetts, A. M.
    To the point.

    Bibliography
    Includes index.
    I. English language—Rhetoric.   2. English language
Grammar—1950-   .   I. Title.
PE1408.T492 1983   808'.042   82–23059
ISBN 0-673-15491-2 (pbk.)

PREFACE

I do two things for a living: write and teach writing. For nearly thirty years, I have been teaching composition, grammar, and usage to college students. As a consultant, I teach business executives, engineers, and other professionals how to write more clearly and accurately.

This little book is written for all those people, and also for anybody who is eavesdropping. I don't believe in slicing up the craft of nonfiction writing into procrustified pieces: *business writing, technical writing, freshman English, medical communication, memos, reports*. These academic classifications are mainly artificial and silly. It's all one, really.

Writing done in any field for any audience should be, as my subtitle suggests, *efficient* and *attractive*. Those who write efficiently do so to make a point; they have a clear sense of organization and direction. They know where they are going, and so does their reader. The writing thus produced is efficient: conveying its message clearly and without fuss. Such writing should also be attractive, drawing the reader in with its liveliness and good sense. The nature of efficient, attractive writing does not change significantly from discipline to discipline or from topic to topic. We are all in the same boat, using the same language.

Then why does my subtitle say "almost any audience"? Because there are those who don't agree with my ideas about clearness and simplicity in writing. Among them, lately, have been a few computer experts and some directors of doctoral dissertations in the social sciences. Be warned. If you write in these areas and follow my advice, you may get into trouble.

Also, that "almost" is a reminder that many truths about most things tend to be partial. For the sake of style, let us agree here to drop all but the most necessary *many's, most's,* and *tends-to-be's* for the remainder of our journey. Let such qualifications be implied. I claim to be no more than 51 percent to 75 percent accurate on the great questions in writing.

Finally:

1. I use the term *essay* throughout to mean any piece of writing that has a beginning, middle, and end—and a *point* to make. For our purposes, an essay can be an interoffice memo, a scientific report, a critical paper on *Hamlet,* a letter to the editor.

2. You will see that occasionally I change format from chapter to chapter (note the differences in four, five, and six). I do this to illustrate certain techniques of organization and visual effect.

3. I have borrowed some of my ideas about argument, persuasion, and audience from Aristotle. The term *argumentative edge* has been used by several authorities, most notably by that fine scholar and writer, Sheridan Baker.

4. In their preface to a book on writing, Deborah Gunther, Lynda Marin, Joan Maxwell, and Jeri Weiss say this on the question of the generic pronoun:

In our opinion good writing is simple and clear. We find it impossible to write simply and clearly while using the very awkward constructions of *he or she, him or her,* and *his or her.* Since the accepted generic singular personal pronouns in the English language are *he, his,* and *him,* we have consciously chosen to employ them in the interest of clarity of style. . . .

As four women who know that the sexes are equal, we ask that you not take our use of the masculine pronoun as a political or philosophical statement.*

I agree.

For helping to shape the manuscript, I thank Harriett Prentiss and Amanda Clark of Scott, Foresman. Thanks particularly to my editor, Kathy Lorden, for helping me to improve it in several important ways.

—A. M. Tibbetts

*From *Writing: A Sourcebook of Exercises & Assignments* by Deborah Gunther, Lynda Marin, Joan Maxwell and Jeri Weiss. Copyright © 1978 by Addison-Wesley Publishing Company, Inc. Reprinted by permission.

CONTENTS

CHAPTER 1

THE ARGUMENTATIVE EDGE

It was early June of 1949, about one o'clock in the afternoon. I was standing in a small pit that I had just finished digging with a shovel. Except that it was only about two feet deep, the pit (whose purpose here is of no consequence) looked like a grave. At that moment— in the early afternoon of a hot Colorado day—I wished it was mine. I was working as a roustabout on an oil exploration crew, twelve hours a day, six to seven days a week. No overtime pay, ever. I was beyond blisters and hope.

Two hours later, I was in the field office gingerly typing a progress letter on a small portable. No shovel. Sitting down. A fan blowing on me. A broken fingernail snapped off, and blood dripped on the typewriter. No matter; reprieve had come. While I had been leaning on a shovel wishing for death, somebody in the Tulsa headquarters had found in my personnel file these lovely words: "Had two years of composition in college," and phoned that information to Colorado. The field crew had nobody who could write English fast and accurately. So for the next five years, I spent hundreds of hours planning, writing, and editing reports in the science of seismic geophysics.

In the three decades since that transfiguration, I have written or edited nonfiction materials on just about any subject you can name. But I'll spare you their naming.

Such has been my education as a writer. Teachers, unquestionably, have been helpful. But I have learned more from other writers and editors, many of them specialists in "non-English" fields like history, business, advertising.

One thing they taught me is that successful pieces of writing in the real world are more alike than different. An accounting report has important similarities to a memo on a problem in geophysics. A theoretical statement on secondary oil recovery is surprisingly like a paper on contemporary novelists. When successful, these pieces of writing tend to use the same basic language, the same rules of grammar, the same "patterns of exposition" (for example, *classifying, contrasting, comparing*). They will even use very similar strategies of paragraphing and organization of large blocks of material. But perhaps the most important similarity lies in one fact: *they are all arguments*.

Early in my career, I had trouble with some of the writing jobs the company threw at me. I was doing from ten to twenty pieces a week; they ranged from highly scientific reports to gossipy stuff for the company magazine. I went to the head of the geophysics department with my tale of woe.

"Well," he said, "try thinking this way. Imagine that every piece you write is an argument that asks a reader to *believe* or *do* something. Or both. Your job is to convince the reader to believe what you want him to, to do what you suggest. Lead him by the hand through your report or letter. When you think he might stumble, stop and find out why, and where you went wrong—because *you* are responsible for keeping him on his feet."

I went away feeling that my mind had been rinsed out with uncommon good sense. I had taken those two years of composition at the university, but no one (as I recall) had ever talked about argument except as a type of writing one took a course in. For example, there was the second-year sequence in composition: a twelve-week quarter each of narration and description, exposition, and argumentation. Nor do I recall any discussion of the reader and his hardships. For my professors I guess he didn't exist. As for the possibility that he might "stumble"—the metaphor opened up a new way of thinking about the difficulties a reader could have in following me over the rhetorical hills and rocks peculiar to scientific work.

But, as it turned out, not so peculiar as I thought. I now have students ranging in age from eighteen to sixty (college freshmen to company presidents), and most of the papers they write are argumentative—they are trying to get people to *believe* or *do* something. Or both.

In effect, my department head's suggestion was that I apply an "argumentative edge" to my writing. I tried it and it worked. Moreover, it has worked on every topic I've ever attacked—from *The Satire of Samuel Johnson* to *Why a Machine Gun Breaks Down*. You employ the argumentative edge on a topic by cutting firmly, even ruthlessly, into its matter, omitting irrelevancies along the way. When you get to the heart of the matter, you stop. The classic introduction, body, and conclusion of an essay are no more than:

1. Tell the reader where you are going to cut the topic
2. Cut till you are finished
3. Stop.

Most of my students tell me they have a hard time getting started. "I've been fiddling around with this piece for a week, and still all I've got are three false starts and a lot of crumpled paper."

I ask: "What's the main point of your argument?" If the student can tell me, my answer is simple: *Start proving that point.* Don't write an "introduction"; just start cutting to the heart of the topic. You may discover that when you have finished writing, you don't need a formal introduction. If you do need one, write it and tack it on.

If the student cannot tell me his main point, I suggest that he ask these questions:

What exactly do you want your reader to think? Believe?

What, if anything, do you want your reader to do? Write (I say) a short but very specific answer to each question. Typical answers look like these:

1. "I want the reader to agree with me that *Macbeth* is not a tragedy."
2. "I want the reader to help me put pressure on the city council to pass a law preventing the burning of leaves in the fall by homeowners."
3. "I want my reader to believe that food stamps are being misused by a significant number of Americans."

4. "I want my reader to accept my plan for buying a word-processing machine for the Public Affairs Department."

Numbers 1 and 3 may require further discussion with the writer; I'll cover such discussion in a later chapter. But 2 and 4 require more discussion and questioning right away:

For 2: Why is burning leaves bad? Will your reader automatically accept your implied premise that it is bad? Do you need to move back a step and write an argument proving just that? In other words, do you need to write Argument A *(need for a change)* before you write Argument B *(call for action)?* Or do you want to try to combine Arguments A and B? This can be done, but it takes more space to develop the arguments convincingly, and the process is more complex.

For 4, the same kind of questioning: Should you write first an Argument A, that there is a need for a change in the Public Affairs Department? If you can't prove a need for a change, proposing one is probably a waste of time. If Argument A is obvious, spend just a little time on it and then charge into Argument B with all flags flying. Argue, convince, persuade.

Of course, for the writer, *persuade* is a transitive verb; there are always readers to be persuaded. And your readership, your audience, can be quite confusedly mixed. A memo to Mr. Jones may be read by five other people—and later acted on by Ms. Smith, a vice-president you never heard of.

Learn to *worry* about your reader! Do you know that I spend more time thinking about *you* (my reader); about how you are reacting; about what you know and don't know; about what interests you and what does not; about your age, experience, and predilections—oh, lord, is *predilections* the right word for *you?* ... To start up my sentence again: I spend more time pondering you and your reactions to my writing than I spend on any other issue—except perhaps the subject of writing itself.

Years ago, I worked with a fine writer who scribbled profiles of his readers. Sometimes a profile ran three or four pages. The rest of us writers wondered why he spent his time this way. He told us, "I must know my readers because I carry on a sort of one-sided dialogue with them":

> *You don't know that word? I'll define it.*
>
> *You disagree that Process Q is more expensive than process Z? I'll supply a paragraph of statistics to prove the point.*
>
> *You're getting bored? I'll see if I can cut some of this section.*
>
> *You wonder whether there aren't solutions to the problem other than the one I mentioned? I'll describe other solutions and tell you why they are weaker than mine.*

Your argumentative edge cuts most cleanly when you present the *relevant facts.* They are perhaps the profoundest part of your message. If you are discussing a short story, quote from it; give the relevant facts about action, characters, and setting. If you are writing a scientific report, give the relevant facts about the experiment, materials used, and variables. I often handle facts with two tools: a typewriter and a pair of sharp scissors. After typing a draft, with the scissors I cut away the unnecessary head or false beginning of the draft, whack off its redundant tail, and perform surgery on the undistinguished parts of its middle. I scissor up to where the facts are. What's left is the argument.

All that I have said is mainly true, but it is not all of the truth. Like other human endeavors, writing has its paradoxes and contradictions. No sooner does an authority say that the writer should always stick to the subject, and not vary from it, and define terms, and give all the facts, and organize in an orderly fashion, than we readers rise up and complain: "This stuff is getting wretchedly dull—give it a rest, will you? Don't you know any jokes?"

No matter what readers may tell you with a perfectly straight face, what they want deep down is an occasional impertinence, digression, or piece of nonsense to alleviate tedium.

And sure enough, a good argument occasionally "impertinates," takes a detour into a little story, pun, or alliterative allusion. These represent the bright colors of the mind and are the legitimate invention of a true writer at work. Gray is dull, and prose that is all gray will make your reader feel a dampness in his soul.

Now I have finished this chapter and will stop.

CHAPTER 2

WORDS TO THINK WITH

Americans have always had their words to live by—words found in the language as fashioned by our uncommon common people. A few examples.

On the day before Christmas, 1775, George Washington wrote to Major General Philip Schuyler:

> When is the time for brave men to exert themselves in the cause of liberty and their country, if this is not? Should any difficulties that they may have to encounter at this important crisis, deter them? God knows, there is not a difficulty, that you both [Schuyler and General Montgomery] very justly complain of, which I have not in an eminent degree experienced, that I am not every day experiencing; but we must bear up against them, and make the best of mankind as they are, since we cannot have them as we wish.

During the Civil War Mary Chesnut, a Southerner, wrote in her diary:

> One begins to understand the power which the ability to vote gives the meanest citizen. We went to one of Uncle Hamilton's splendid dinners, plate, glass, china, and everything that was nice to eat. In the piazza, when the

gentlemen were smoking after dinner, in the midst of them sat Squire MacDonald, the well-digger. He was officiating in that capacity at Plain Hill, and apparently he was most at his ease of all. He had his clay pipe in his mouth, he was cooler than the rest, being in his shirt sleeves, and he leaned back luxuriously in his chair tilted on its two hind legs, with his naked feet up on the bannister. Said Louisa—"Look, the mud from the well is sticking through his toes! See how solemnly polite and attentive Mr. Chesnut is to him?" "Oh, that's his way. The raggeder and more squalid the creature, the more polite and the softer Mr. Chesnut grows."—*A Diary from Dixie*

Late in the nineteenth century, a country physician wrote to a woman about her tubercular husband: "My advice is short, but I know it is good. Tell him to dismiss all thoughts of curing his lungs; it can't be done, never could be, never will be by way of lung remedies. Nature will cure them if she can. No doctor can."

In 1937, Richard Wright published these words:

I now saw a world leap to life before my eyes because I could explore it, and that meant not going home when school was out, but wandering, watching, asking, talking. Had I gone home to eat my plate of greens, Granny would not have allowed me out again, so the penalty I paid for roaming was to forfeit my food for twelve hours. I would eat mush at eight in the morning and greens at seven or later at night. To starve in order to learn about my environment was irrational, but so were my hungers. With my books slung over my shoulder, I would tramp with a gang into the woods, to rivers, to creeks, into the business district, to the doors of poolrooms, into the movies when we could slip in without paying, to neighborhood ball games, to brick kilns, to lumberyards, to cottonseed mills to watch men work. There were hours when hunger would make me weak, would make me sway while walking, would make my heart give a sudden wild spurt of beating that would shake my body and make me breathless; but the happiness of being free would lift me beyond hunger, would enable me to discipline the sensations of my body to the extent that I could temporarily forget.—*Black Boy*

In 1955, an American scientist wrote in a technical report:

The Adams Prospect looks good—when you first look at it. The [seismic] records appear fairly easy to interpret. They show a long, narrow high running north and south with a closure of about 120 feet. That's a lot of structure for this area, particularly in the Cretaceous beds. But when you consider the location of producing wells in the area, you begin to wonder whether somebody hasn't made a mistake on the Adams Prospect. Consider, for example, that the Cretaceous reflector changes character radically from shothole 23 to shothole 70. . . .

Who said that writers in science or engineering have to use big words and impenetrable jargon?

In the last couple of pages, you have read the words of a man who became general of the army and later president of the United States; a white woman from the South; a country physician from Colorado; a black man who rose from poverty to become a famous writer; a modern scientist well known in his field. Their writing helps to show that the words we Americans really live by have certain major characteristics. They are clear, accurate, and (often) simple. It matters little whether the writer is man or woman, whether the subject is trivial or important, technical or complex. Apart from the special terms necessary in every discipline or trade, no special language or type of rhetoric is needed for people in different occupations. The psychologist, mechanic, lawyer, carpenter, or chemist can and should use plain words.

Anybody who tells you differently has probably got his hand in your pocket. Typically he will have an idea to sell that is weak enough he must use jargon to conceal its weakness. So you and I—and perhaps a few other people (sometimes a whole nationful of them)—go confusedly round and round trying to figure out what to think about his idea. This is the major problem with jargon, and also with gobbledygook and verbal nonsense of every kind: *You can't think in it.* G. K. Chesterton wrote:

> If you say *The social utility of the indeterminate sentence is recognized by all criminologists as part of our sociological evolution towards a more humane and scientific view of punishment,* you can go on talking like that for hours with hardly a movement of the gray matter inside your skull. But if you begin, *I wish Jones to go to jail and Brown to say when Jones shall come out,* you will discover, with a thrill of horror, that you are obliged to think.—*Orthodoxy*

Words to live by are those which allow, encourage, *oblige* us to think. The words in the column on the left prevent thought; they are a form of mental anesthetic; they numb the mind.

Numbs the mind	Makes us think
You will suffer disciplinary incarceration.	You will stay after school.
Your choice of jewelry is very individual.	That pin is the wrong color.

They are utilizing their personnel maximally.	They are using their workers very well.
Sinistrality in a woman is a developmental anomaly of preferred laterality.	A woman is left-handed because. . . .
My specific function has been minimized.	I don't do much.
Your concept is marginally relevant.	Your idea won't work.
This machine is not cost-efficient.	This machine is cheap to make but expensive to operate.
The social upsurges have been caused by indefinite governing factors.	? ? ? (I give up.)

That jargon in the left column has several causes. One is carelessness. Another is the desire to sound important. A third is striving for verbal precision or exactness where it is not needed. Here is an example of *fake precision.* I had a graduate student in agriculture who did research on the living conditions of pigs. He wrote a paper for publication concluding that "pig *microspace* affects *short-term amiability.*" Translated: If you put too many pigs in a small space, they fight.

A fourth case of jargon is the desire to be in the know and with it. In order to be fashionable, one wears the latest width in neckties, dances the latest steps, and burbles the latest in bafflegab:

I'm *into* really *parenting* my kids.

Given their *life-style,* they need a *meaningful relationship.*

Hopefully, her office won't need *massive restructuring.*

Such *fad words* sneak into society like a flu bug. One week we are all feeling fine and the next we are sniffling and throwing up. *Parenting* appeared one day a few years ago. In less than a month it could be seen infecting newspaper columnists; later, magazine writers. After six months, books went on sale with titles like *Parenting as a Science of Interpersonal Relations.*

The final cause of jargon is the all-too-human lust for keeping secrets and thereby maintaining power over others. Members of the professions (and of some trades) use jargon as a weapon. The mumbo-jumbo of lawyers, for example, keeps us in thrall to them. I asked a fancy oral surgeon whether my daughter's wisdom teeth should be removed. He said: "An operation is not contraindicated." That surgeon had me by the throat—and the pocketbook.

Have you noticed that some people working for the airlines speak so you can't understand them? Secrecy, prestige, power. That is what the airline pilot has and every baggage handler yearns for. It is funny, though, when the airline wizard reaches into his bag of verbal tricks only to produce something like this sign, prominently placed in the restroom of an airplane two of us were traveling in:

Please do not throw foreign articles into flushing toilet.

The lady I customarily fly with returned to her seat, borrowed my pen, and produced this letter to the president of the airline:

I read your instructions in the restroom and at first did more or less what you requested. But now I am not sure I followed the instructions properly. If the toilet is not flushing, can I throw foreign articles into it? *Flushing toilet* implies that, as it were, nobody pulls the chain. Do your toilets flush by themselves? Also can I throw a *native* article into one of your toilets, flushing or otherwise?

Anyhow, trying to obey your sign, I later went forward in the airplane (that which your pilots ingenuously call the *aircraft),* grabbed a small OPEC executive—indeed a nasty foreign article—and threw him into the toilet which was, for the moment, nonflushing.

I hope I have done right.

/signed/   Confused

Did my fellow flyer's letter to the president of the airline make him think?

Let us hope so.

CHAPTER 3

GETTING STARTED— HOOK YOUR SUBJECT

Have you noticed how good writers often use a title to help shape a paper or essay? H. W. Fowler called an essay on English usage "Out of the Frying Pan." It was a piece about how writers, in trying to avoid an awkward construction, create one that is worse: ". . . and into the fire." A good title may have one (or two or three) *shaping* terms that help you control your paper. Wilfred Sheed titled an article: "We *Overrate* Love." Senator Daniel Moynihan called an essay: "Politics as the Art of the *Impossible*."

Titles do at least two things. They tell the reader what the piece is about. And they provide a *hook* to hang the writer's ideas on. My wife Charlene teaches composition. One winter she taught a graduate student who had a terrible time starting to write. He was a high-school principal on sabbatical; his thesis subject was educational administration. He showed Charlene a dozen pages of false starts. She read them and asked: "How many subjects have you got here?" The student said: "That's part of the problem. I've got so much to say that I don't know where to begin. If I could just get started. . . ." Charlene pointed to the back of the room. Along the wall was a line of coat hooks, and his coat was hanging on one of them.

"Look at your coat," Charlene said. "When you came in, you didn't throw your coat at the wall and hope it would miraculously stay up there off the floor. You hung it high and dry on a hook. You're trying to throw your paper at a rhetorical wall, hoping it will stay there; but your subject keeps falling down in a heap. Try some hooks. For example: *Why school principals fail.* The hook is provided in the words *why* and *fail.* As you write, keep hanging your ideas on those two words." Charlene told him of other possible hooks in these titles:

The *Successful* Principal *Listens*
How a *Good* Principal *Prepares*
A *Good* Principal is *Lucky*
The *Principal* and Town *Politics*
Should *You* Be a School *Principal?*

The last title has the hooks *you* and *principal,* with the added control of a question. The point of the paper is implied in the question, which can be answered in several ways. Charlene told the student: "Now provide another hook for your paper, something like the phrase *qualities of leadership.* In your introduction to the paper, start to answer the question in the title by telling readers that they can be *successful school principals* if they have certain *qualities of leadership.*"

This chapter you are reading is hooked on three words—*getting started* and *hook.* As I develop the ideas these words suggest, I am trying to convince you that even though writing is an enigmatic art, you can find processes in it. One of these is the hooking process, which makes the planning stage easier and also helps you to stay on the subject once you have started.

Your hooks can be part of the *thesis* or *thesis sentence*. Examples:

> Because some residents are *allergic* to the smoke, the city should *ban* all leaf burning.

> Although word-processors are splendid *toys*, they *waste* a company's *money*.

> The *geophysical* evidence on X Prospect is too *weak* to base *geological* conclusions on.

I do not customarily employ a thesis sentence unless the material is complex. Some topics are intractable, even violently uncooperative. You have to grab them and hold them down—put them in the straitjacket of a thesis sentence. Once they are docile you can figure out a way to manage them.

In any event, I keep my hooks sharp, and am careful to hang most ideas on them. Readers do not usually appreciate irrelevancy. Yet if I find my composition becoming irrelevant *and* informative or interesting, I may go back and change the hooks to fit the new material. An idea will sometimes come to vivid life and demand to be heard: "Hey! I'm going to run off this way—I'll lead, you follow!" If I can spare the time I will follow the idea. Who knows what fabulous riches lie just over the next rhetorical hill?

Good writing occasionally surprises (see Chapter 6), and at points along the way the writer can be just as surprised as the reader. One imagines that Paul Colinvaux felt a small unexpected thrill when this book title popped into his mind: *Why Big Fierce Animals Are*

Rare. The hooks in his title are well honed, while the hooks in his subtitle give more control over the subject: *An Ecologist's Perspective.* With hooks like those, once Colinvaux started writing how could he stop?

So when you pick a topic (or it is picked for you), walk around it looking for things to hang your argument on:

> A *boat* is a hole in the water surrounded by wood into which one *pours money.*

> *Sex* is one of the few skills people learn through *talk* and not *demonstration.* Can you imagine what it would be like if a couple of nervous parents sat their child down in the living room and tried to *explain* how to swim?—Eleanor Hamilton, marriage counselor

Let's return to those topics which are complex or uncooperative, those you may need a straitjacket for. Besides the thesis sentence, here is another device for dealing with them.

Have you ever tried to hold on to a soapy, plump baby? When my son John was little, I used to give him his daily bath. He was a fat but compact little fellow, with round firm surfaces and a center of gravity that defied the laws of physics. And he wiggled a great deal. Halfway through his bath, he always became impossible to hang on to. I used to lose him two or three times every night. He would go galoomph into the water while I was reaching one-handedly for a towel; or while I was scrubbing away he would slowly disappear under the surface, only to arise howling when I managed to find a handle: foot, hand, or ear. Eventually I solved John's problem by washing him geographically, peninsula by peninsula.

You can handle a slippery writing topic as I did my son, a part at a time—in the case of the topic, a hook at a time.

Problem: You must write an essay on Jonathan Swift's *Fourth Voyage* in *Gulliver's Travels,* a short but complex narrative satire. You can't deal with all the issues in the *Voyage* at once, so you employ four hooks:

1. Plot
2. Characterization
3. Theme
4. Style

Your thesis hooks are in this sentence: "The *Fourth Voyage* is brilliant in *style* and *theme* but deficient in *characterization* and *plot*." One can disagree with that thesis; but then critics have been disagreeing about the *Fourth Voyage* for more than two hundred fifty years.

Now the question is, how can you organize a paper after you have hooked its subject? I'll suggest a few methods in the next chapter.

CHAPTER 4

ORGANIZING: FIND A *SHAPE* FOR YOUR ESSAY

To oversimplify for a moment, there are two kinds of writers—those who like outlines and those who don't.

Stephen Jay Gould is Professor of Geology at Harvard University. In 1980 his columns in *Natural History* won the National Magazine Award for Essays and Criticism. In 1981 his book, *The Panda's Thumb,* won the American Book Award for science. Here is what Gould says about outlines (for his columns in *Natural History* he produces a paragraph-by-paragraph outline):

> I really do believe outlines exist in heaven. I'm a Platonist when it comes to articles. I really believe there is a correct organization for each article. Once you find it, everything fits in.

Jacques Barzun has had a brilliant career as Professor of History, Provost of Columbia University, and writer extraordinary. He has published over two dozen books, several of them on writing and English usage. His opinion of outlines:

Well, for my taste, outlines are useless, fettering, im-
becile. Sometimes, when you get into a state of anarchy,
or find yourself writing in circles, it may help to jot down
a sketchy outline of the topics (or in a story, of the phases)
so far covered. You outline, in short, something that
already exists in written form, and this may help to show
where you started backstitching.—*On Writing, Editing,
and Publishing*

As I said, to suggest that writers are either outliners
or anti-outliners is an oversimplification. One reason is
that *outline* is an ambiguous term. It can mean a few
jottings on scrap paper, or a detailed piece of formal ar-
chitecture covering several pages and with every
roman numeral, arabic number, and upper- and lower-
case letter reverently placed in its assigned niche. If we
accept both meanings, then certainly every writer
outlines at one time or another, if only in his head.

What should we believe about the value of outlines?
The lengthy formal outline is a tool which you may use
if the situation warrants and if you find such outlining
a comfortable way to organize. My writer-wife finds
the formal outline comfortable; I usually do not. But
on occasion I have used it—before, during, and after
writing. *After writing* when I didn't know where I had
been. When you are desperate, you grasp at any straw.

One straw I have grasped on many occasions: the
organize-by-card method. I gather all my materials and
data, reduce them to a number of "single ideas," which
are put on cards, *one idea to a card:*

Kinds of reader   (first card)
Kinds of writer   (second card)
Appealing styles   (third card)
Unappealing styles   (fourth card)
etc., etc.

Depending on the subject and the length of the piece I am working on, I may have six cards or sixty. Once, for a book, I had several thousand.

I start organizing an essay by shuffling the cards, eventually laying them out on a large flat surface: table, bed, or floor. I classify the cards by subject; that is, by title and subtitle. I move the cards—*and their single ideas*—around: forward, backward, sideways. I try various orderings: from the simple to the complex; from the little to the big; from the early to the late (time sequence); from the cause to the effect.

I keep doing this until a pattern begins to appear— what I call a *shape*. This is the overall organization that best fits my material, approach to it, and reader. In other words, I try to let subject and shape—with help from me—find each other. When they succeed in their search, I am ready to write, but usually without benefit of a long formal outline.

First, I agree with Jacques Barzun that a formal outline is often "fettering." It can produce manacles on the mind. Second, and more important, the typical outline has so many trees in it I can't find the forest. One writes an outline from the top down. By the time I get to the middle of it (perhaps in point III., B., 2. (a)), I don't know where the devil I am. The detailed outline seems to be a subject unto itself, a country with its own king and elaborate set of laws.

Because I intend to be king of my rhetorical country, I write—*draw*—my organizational shape on a single sheet of scratch paper so that I can keep it under surveillance at all times. This sheet is tacked on the wall over my typewriter so I can refer to it easily.

For example, suppose I want to write a piece on why so many touring bikers, fanatics who love riding their ten-speeds for hours on end, get damaged knees.

Severe knee-damage from biking is no joke; it can last for life. I start organizing the subject by putting single ideas on four-by-six-inch index cards and doodling on scratch paper. After messing around for a while, I decide to hook the subject on "macho-ism," and to give a number of causes of knee problems. Still working on a shape, I doodle some more:

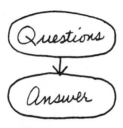

After reading my index cards again, and rearranging them, I try refining my first shape into:

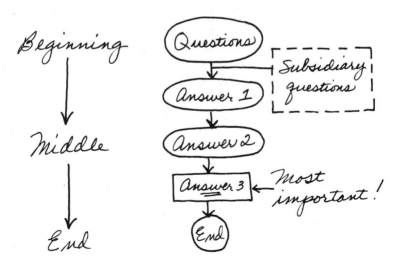

Now I have a completed shape that fits my material:

CONTENT
OF
SHAPE

QUESTION:	Why do some bikers get sore knees?
SUBSIDIARY QUESTIONS:	(will mention, but won't elaborate): Age of biker? Type of bike? Difficulty of terrain covered?
ANSWER 1:	Biker does not gear down on hills.
ANSWER 2:	Biker tries to ride too long (8 to 10 hours).
ANSWER 3:	Psychological, most important: Biker is macho and foolishly competitive; must win over other bikers at all costs, even though racing as such is not involved.

So far, I have emphasized the fact that *shape* and *subject* have a special relation to each other. Now, to take the problem by a different handle, let's discuss the common organizational shapes that are available. Remember that these are suggested shapes only. They are not carved in granite.

Do you want your reader to act? Try an *action shape.*

Do you want your reader to understand an idea or "thing"? Use a *definition shape.*

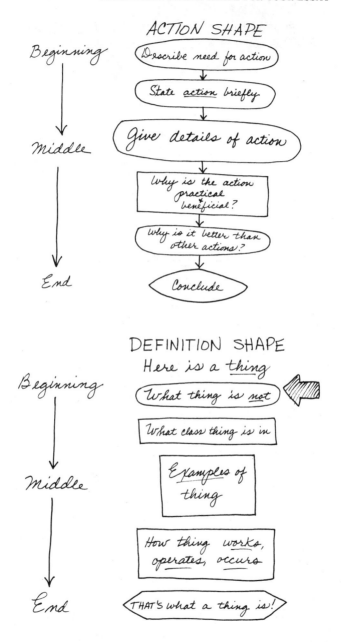

ACTION SHAPE

Beginning
- Describe need for action
- State *action* briefly

Middle
- Give details of action
- Why is the action practical & beneficial?
- Why is it better than other actions?

End
- Conclude

DEFINITION SHAPE

Beginning
- Here is a *thing*
- What thing is *not*
- What class thing is in

Middle
- Examples of thing
- How thing *works*, *operates*, *occurs*

End
- THAT'S what a thing is!

Do you want your reader to agree with the results of your experiment? Consider Report Shape I.

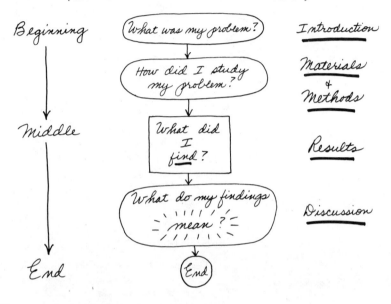

REPORT SHAPE I (EXPERIMENT)

Beginning — What was my problem? — *Introduction*

How did I study my problem? — *Materials & Methods*

Middle — What did I find? — *Results*

What do my findings mean? — *Discussion*

End — End

This is the shape for scientific papers that is recommended by Robert A. Day, who for 20 years has been managing editor of the American Society for Microbiology. For many such papers, it is a convenient formulaic shape. But I have written or edited papers in science and engineering that employed somewhat different shapes to good effect.

Here is another report shape, as suggested by Melba Murray, an internationally known authority on communication. It follows the pattern of *What? Why? How? Now what?*

REPORT SHAPE II

(Can be used by engineers & business people)

➤ I've got some _news_ for you! *

    What do I recommend? (Details)

    Why do I recommend this? (Details)

    How do I know the recommendation

        is good? (Details)

      Now what??

[How do we act on the recommendation?]

* Don't _bury_ the news!

I don't want to suggest that for every subject or method of influencing your reader there is a special organizational shape. This is like believing that for every offensive setup in football there is a special defense that always works. It is true that some shapes are widely applicable and can be used time and again. For example, I often use the action shape. It is an old strategy; the ancient Greeks and Romans knew and taught it. For many writing problems it works well.

But, like most writers, I just as often develop a particular shape for the situation. For instance, I have recently been asked by a company to comment on five proposals for improving the flow of written material through its various operating units. After investigation I decided that two proposals have little merit, but that three are worth looking into. Here is the shape for the report I'll write:

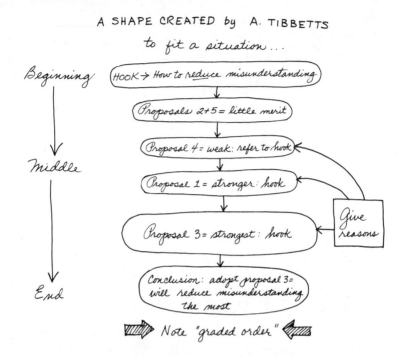

A SHAPE CREATED by A. TIBBETTS
to fit a situation ...

Beginning — HOOK → How to reduce misunderstanding

Proposals 2+5 = little merit

Middle — Proposal 4 = weak: refer to hook

Proposal 1 = stronger: hook

Give reasons

Proposal 3 = strongest: hook

End — Conclusion: adopt proposal 3 = will reduce misunderstanding the most

Note "graded order"

I created this shape after considering all the elements in the situation:

My reader (actually several readers—it's an old rule in report writing *that the reader addressed is almost never the only reader*)

The nature of the material

My hook

The specific action I suggested (the point of the argument)

Before we turn to another question in organization, one useful shape deserves mention. This is the shape of *graded order,* which I have just used in Report Shape

II. Graded order can be applied to many different kinds of material. For example, you can order or arrange your ideas from the "little" to the "big":

GRADED ORDER

Little least expensive   least workable   least pleasing
↕   ↕   ↕
more   "   more   "   more   "
↓
Big   most   "   most   "   most   "

Note: On some topics, you can use the graded order of *big to little*.

To conclude:

1. Every successful essay has an organization or *shape* of some kind. Shapes can vary considerably, but there are only a few basic ones.
2. Your reader must have a hint, however slight, of the shape you are using. (More of this in the next chapter.) If you wish, you can give more than just a hint of the shape: "I will define the XYZ Process, and give three reasons why it is too costly to use at this time."
3. When you set up an expectation in the reader about a shape, be sure you fulfill it.
4. Certain materials suggest—even demand—their own shapes. By contrast, some materials are so complex or downright troublesome that you have to force a shape on them.

CHAPTER 5

TAKE YOUR READER BY THE HAND

Losing your reader on the page is easy. You know where you are going, but he does not. Your reader is a traveler in an unfamiliar land whose only hope is to make it from one landmark to another, from a scratched rock to a blazed tree.

As writer, you lead; as reader, he follows. In hints and signs you tell him how to follow.

USE THE PROMISE PATTERN

In the *promise pattern*, you make a bargain with your reader. You promise to tell him something, and then you fulfill the promise. In paragraphs, promises are typically made at or near the beginning:

These few examples make one thing clear: for anyone who has to survive in the desert, the heat of the day, both cause and effect of the lack of water, is the chief danger. *Temperatures reach an amazing height.* In Baghdad

PROMISE MADE

PROMISE
FULFILLED
BY
EXAMPLES
AND
DETAILS

the thermometer in the hot summer months often climbs to 150°F., occasionally even to 180° and over (in the sun). In the Sahara near Azizia (Libya) temperatures of 134° in the shade have been recorded, and in July 1913 that was also the temperature in the Great Salt Lake Desert (also in the shade). But if the thermometer is put in the sand there at noon during the summer, the mercury goes up to 176°. On the side of Highway 91, which goes through the Mohave Desert, it has sometimes been 140° in the shade at noon; in the evenings the thermometer sinks to a "low" of 90°. In Libya, Montgomery's and Rommel's soldiers sometimes fried eggs on the armor plate of their tanks.—Cord-Christian Troebst, *The Art of Survival*

In essays of more than one paragraph, you will make promises when necessary as you develop your argument. An essay of fifteen paragraphs could have ten, twelve, fourteen promises; but probably no more than fourteen because you can't promise more than you can fulfill. Conclusions seldom promise.

A paragraph, it should be stressed, is several devices at once—a unit of thought, a method of thesis development, a "resting place" for the reader. But long, unbroken paragraphs can put a reader to sleep.

In books, you will find promises within promises. The chapters—big self-confident promises—are usually well defined; they even have their own titles. In the typical essay, however, the pattern of promises fulfills its bargain with the reader more or less as shown in the diagram on page 32.

The "promise" in the pattern may often act much like topic sentences. But topic sentences are partly

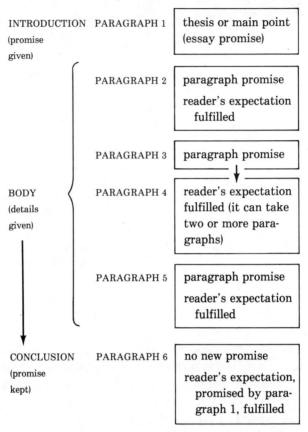

mythical beasts. Textbooks demand that students use them, but experienced writers often don't. Instead they keep saying to the reader (for example): *Here is a useful objection to the theory of XYZ.* Then they tell what the objection is. Moreover, unlike the topic sentence, the promise may take two or three sentences to state.

June Kronholz, a staff reporter for the *Wall Street Journal,* wrote a front-page story, part of which you see below. The spaced periods indicate my cuts of large batches of material. Try putting a piece of paper over the passage and forcing yourself to read one line at a time. How much does Kronholz promise you—and where are her promises made?

> ZAMBEZI RIVER, Zimbabwe—This is a story about power, sex, predation and violence in Africa.
>
> It's about crocodiles.
>
> First, the power. A crocodile can grow to a length of 20 feet, weigh half a ton and tackle a 900-pound buffalo that wanders past at lunchtime. . . .
>
> Now for the sex. A crocodile reaches maturity when he is 2.5 feet long, which can take anywhere from 10 to 20 years, depending on how well he has been eating. . . .
>
> Here's where the predation comes in. An adult crocodile has only one predator: a man with a rifle (a Soviet-designed AK-47 is preferred in these parts). . . .
>
> Now, finally, the violence. Given the choice between a man and a buffalo, a crocodile almost always will opt for a fish. But occasionally a man will happen along the river bank. . . .

Although I cut more than 90 percent of the article, you can still see how Kronholz uses the promise pattern. Her reader can tell where she is going, and can easily follow the trail she laid down. Because it predicts the direction you are taking in your essay, because it marks the trail ahead, the promise pattern is a major device for keeping your reader following happily close behind you.

Perhaps I can dramatize this by inserting here a typed page of mine just rescued from the trash can. These are two rotten paragraphs I threw away when I was trying to find a lead for this chapter.

> If you have found the right organizational shape for your essay (see the last chapter), you will find that your organizational problems are solved. For once the "big strategies" are found, your essay will write itself. Every-

thing is now logically arranged, and one part will flow into another. Your worries are over.

But even though such advice contains considerable truth, my editor would never let me get away with it. Editors, may I add, if they are any good, will give you a lingering pain behind the eyes; but it is necessary pain. Always be nice to your editor. He—now, blessedly often, she—will pick you up when you fall flat, dust you off, and set you straight on the road again. Your editor will repair your syntax, erase your stupidities, and make you rich—if not in money then in the esteem of your readers.

Taken idea by idea, the material here is not all bad. But you would have been confused if I had let the paragraphs stand. With the last sentence of paragraph 1, I pretended to lead you in a certain direction. But at the start of paragraph 2, I obliterated that trail and went off 180° in another direction without warning. In the middle of paragraph 2, I started marking yet another trail and then quit, again without warning. Now you are lost and irritable. I made several promises to you about where this chapter is going, and broke all of them.

USE HEADINGS (WHEN APPROPRIATE)

The heading is a splendid device for blazing a prose trail. Keep them specific and as short as possible. Can you improve any of my headings in this chapter?

MAKE YOUR INTRODUCTION PREDICT

Once you have decided on a shape for your essay (see Chapter 4), you are prepared to make predictions for your reader. As you start writing, consider how best to make them. For example, you might start a company memo in this way:

As you know, the company has planned to open the north wing of the old plant to make a recreation hall for employees. But I have recently learned that the cost of renovation will be twice as high as expected. So I am suggesting that the Recreation Committee look into moving our packing and mailing center out of the south wing and into the north wing. We could then use the center's space, which would require little renovation. [Rest of memo omitted.]

Now put yourself in the reader's place:

Content of the introduction	What the reader expects
"As you know . . . "	Something is coming that I have heard about before.
"But . . . "	An objection is coming.
" . . . I have recently learned that the cost of renovation will be twice as high as expected."	Later in the memo I will get some specific cost figures to show this comparison.
"So . . . "	The writer is going to make a cause-effect judgment.
" . . . I am suggesting that the Recreation Committee look into moving our packing and mailing center out of the south wing and into the north wing. We could then use the center's space, which would require little renovation."	I expect facts on the two wings (size, facilities, etc.), and on the lower costs of renovation. I also expect proof of lower costs for the entire operation.

As a test of how introductions predict, you might take a few minutes to look at the first few sentences of typical essays, reports, letters, editorials, etc. Or skim the first few sentences of several chapters in this book. Chapter Four, for instance, starts:

Content of the introduction	What the reader expects
"To oversimplify for a moment . . . "	I expect a statement that needs qualification.
" . . . there are two kinds of writers. . . "	I expect a classification.
" . . . those who like outlines and those who don't."	I expect a discussion of the advantages and disadvantages of outlining.

A single sentence can predict both content and "type of communication." Note how much (and how differently) these introductory sentences predict:

Gawain T. Finfrock prowled his corner of the outfield like a great jungle cat: heavy, even ponderous, yet lithe and graceful.

Professor Gawain T. Finfrock was dead, murdered (it seemed) by his own parakeet.

As the medical examiner assigned to the case, I performed a routine autopsy on the body of Gawain T. Finfrock.

I, Gawain T. Finfrock, being of sound mind. . . .

Gawain T. Finfrock's production of *The Pirates of Penzance* is flawed in three serious ways.

If Dean Gawain T. Finfrock wishes to improve his administration of the College, he should. . . .

> In contrast to Howard Hughes, Gawain T. Finfrock—the noted philanthropist—always gave money to. . . .

An introductory paragraph, even a short one, can promise and predict:

> Contrary to any rumors you may have heard, the price for Bertolucci's *Last Tango in Paris* is just right—$5 a ticket, the going rate for pornographic films. For make no bones about it, *Last Tango in Paris* is pornography.—Joy Gould Boyum

USE THE "DOUBLE SIGNPOST"

When you come to a corner of your prose trail, mark it with a *double signpost,* which points back to where you've been and forward to where you're going:

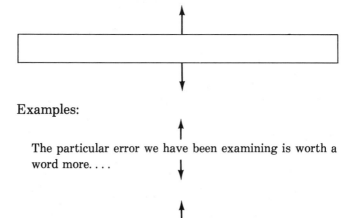

Examples:

> The particular error we have been examining is worth a word more. . . .

> To this intense moralism there was added in the Middle Ages a ready belief in the occurrence of the supernatural on earth—Jacques Barzun and Henry Graff, *The Modern Researcher*

USE ECHOES AND REPEATED WORDS

If you are a typical American, you have been taught in school to avoid verbal repetition, which, for some reason, many teachers consider a sin. Yet carefully repeating key words and phrases helps your reader to stay on course. Also helpful are "echoes"—synonyms or other words that remind your reader of the essay's theme. Here is a good example, written by Professor Moses Hadas, Jay Professor of Greek at Columbia University. Note the repetition and echo of *ritual* and *ceremony:*

> From his first hour of life, when he was laid at his father's feet for *ceremonial acceptance,* the Roman lived in *a world of order* and *ritual.* He was, above all else, a *traditionalist,* a man who acknowledged change only grudgingly, and in domestic and social life hardly at all. Thus, while Rome itself was changing from a small city-state into a vast empire, its people maintained *the old ceremonies* and *customs almost unaltered.*

I skip five paragraphs to Hadas' discussion of marriage:

> Once the match had been made, the betrothal was formalized in a *ritual.* At this *ceremony* the dowry was stipulated, and the bride-to-be, usually 14 or 15, received gifts and a pledge of marriage from her fiancé. Symbolic of this pledge was a metal ring worn on the third finger of her hand, from which a nerve was believed to lead directly to the heart.
>
> Of the three different forms of marriage in vogue at the time of the early Empire, the most *formal,* used only by patricians, was the *confarreatio.* Under this contract, the woman's person and property were surrendered to her husband. For women who demanded greater freedom

from their husbands, there were other, less rigid forms of marriage. In the *coemptio,* the groom symbolically "bought" the bride from herself. In the *usus,* somewhat similar to modern commonlaw marriages, the couple would agree to live as man and wife without any religious *ceremony.* After a year they were considered legally married. In such an alliance the woman might actually retain rights to property she owned—provided she absented herself from her husband's bed and board for three nights every year.

Weddings—especially the *confarreatio* form—were *rich in ceremonial.* The date was selected with care: many days of the year, including all of March and May and half of June, were considered unlucky. On the eve of the big day, the bride dedicated her childhood dress and toys to the household gods of her father. On the day of her wedding she attired herself in a special tunic, fastened about her waist by a woolen girdle in a "Hercules knot," which only the groom might untie. Over this she wore a saffron cloak and veil of flaming orange. Her hair was arranged in an elaborate six-plaited coiffure, topped by a crown of flowers.—*Imperial Rome*

USE TRANSITIONAL WORDS AND PHRASES

The simplest and most obvious transitions are those that count in order: "This is my *first* idea. . . . Now for the *second* idea. . . . *Third,* there is. . . . " Less obvious are those transitions that do not so much lead the reader by the hand as smooth his way: "*It is certain that* the reactor could not have blown up so easily if. . . . *While this was going on,* the men in the black suits were blowing up the bridge. . . . *Moreover,* the two physicists could not agree on what to do."

Here are some typical transitional words and phrases:

To explain ideas: *for instance, for example, such as, specifically, in particular, to illustrate, thus*

To count or separate ideas: *first, second, third* (but not *firstly, secondly, thirdly*), *moreover, in addition, another, furthermore, also, again, finally*

To compare ideas: *likewise, similarly, in the same way*

To contrast or qualify ideas: *however, on the other hand, on the contrary, but*

To show cause or effect: *as a result, consequently, therefore, thus*

Such a listing could continue indefinitely, for under special circumstances hundreds of words and phrases that are not ordinarily considered transitional can be used to link words, ideas, or sentences. As a small example, here is a short passage taken from the middle of a book (transitional words and phrases are in capitals):

IT IS EVIDENT THAT the little words of English constitute a kind of inner voice—a language within a language—capable of understudying most of the flashier ornaments of *The Oxford English Dictionary* and *Webster's New International Dictionary, Unabridged.* They can be of enormous value to the English novitiate because they cover so much ground; each one pinch-hits for hundreds of bigger, if subtler, words; and they are simple to spell and pronounce. BUT their simplicity is deceptive. They can be used in so many ways that their very versatility sometimes creates confusion in the mind of the learner. THIS is the "masked complexity" which the foreign student may discover when he looks more closely at the apparently innocuous alliance of little verbs and little prepositions.

Contemplate, FOR EXAMPLE, the little word *up.* What is it? Most of the time it behaves like a preposition, indicating direction *(He lives up the street)*. BUT it can ALSO masquerade as an adverb *(It's time to get up)*; a noun *(Every life has its ups and downs)*; a verb *(I'll up you five dollars)*; or an adjective *(The sun is up)*. IN ADDITION TO its multiple function in the combination *give up*, it plays a ubiquitous and sometimes superfluous role in a variety of other expressions, SUCH AS *add up, clean up, do up, drink up, hurry up*. . . . To the foreign student it seems paradoxical THAT THE SAME MEANING is conveyed by *His house burned up* and *His house burned down*. . . . EVEN MORE BEWILDERING are those situations where utterly unrelated concepts are evoked by one and the same phrase—e.g. *makes up*, whose transient meaning depends on whether the context is cosmetics *(She takes an hour to make up her face)*; indecision *(I just can't make up my mind)*; domesticity *(Let's make up the bed)*; forgiveness *(Kiss and make up)*; fiction *(I'll make up some kind of a story)*; or atonement *(Some day I'll make up for this mistake)*.—Lincoln Barnett, *The Treasure of Our Tongue*

CONCLUSION

As a test of the ideas in this chapter, you might try this little experiment: Pick out a page in the middle of any well written article or book. On that page, underline all the words and phrases (even sentences) that represent the devices for keeping a reader on track. Now, using a felt-tip pen, blot out all the words you have underlined. (If your material is too valuable to do this, stick the page on a photocopy machine before blotting. Or, have someone type it, omitting all the underlined words.) Now put the page aside for a week or so.

When you pick up the page after a week, how easily can you read and understand it? A certain rule of thumb often applies: The clearer the original writing, the odder and more disorganized the blotted version will seem. As the reader, you have become a stranger in a strange land.

CHAPTER 6

HOW TO MOVE THROUGH A SENTENCE

Writing has motion. In the larger blocks of writing (like paragraphs), you move down the page, carrying your reader with you:

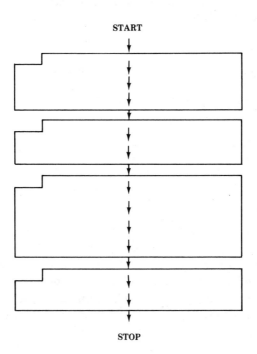

But for the all-important smaller block of writing—the sentence—you move across the page, from left to right:

Capital letter $\rightarrow$ $\rightarrow$ $\rightarrow$ $\rightarrow$ *period. Capital letter* $\rightarrow$ $\rightarrow$ $\rightarrow$ $\rightarrow$ *period. Capital letter* $\rightarrow$ $\rightarrow$ $\rightarrow$ $\rightarrow$ $\rightarrow$ $\rightarrow$ $\rightarrow$ *period.*

On a page of writing, writer and reader move in two directions: *down* and *across*. It is impossible to say which motion requires more skill from the writer. Certainly each is necessary for communication. In each kind the reader must follow your lead. He may have the most trouble following your sentence across the page. Unquestionably, the sentence (our subject for the rest of this chapter) is a tricky thing. Whole books are written on it—its grammar, syntax, rhetoric—and on how to manage it. We will hit only the high spots of sentence-writing.

As you scan it on the page, line by line, a sentence is made of small narrow objects a few inches long and less than one-quarter-inch high:

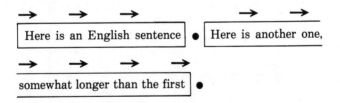

It is greatly to your advantage that sentences are put in these narrow rigid spaces. The ideas thus imprisoned can be manipulated—combined, separated, shortened, lengthened, switched, taken out, put in. The rigidity of the space forces the sentence to keep its basic outer form, but you as writer control almost everything else about it.

A part of your control over the sentence is made possible by its motion, from left to right. "Dog cat the a bit" is meaningless, but "The dog bit a cat" makes sense. Thus you and your reader have something essential in common. You both start at the left of the sentence, and fight your way rightwards through its narrow prison:

You and your reader are imprisoned together. The more the two of you cooperate, the more you can move together through the complex masses of verbal symbols and levels of the "code" that we call writing.

This cooperation is accomplished partly by *prediction*. That is, you supply what your reader predicts. Suppose you write:

The _____ said something _____ when she _____ her thumb with a _____.

Because the reader is familiar with the sentence code, he can rather easily predict what kinds of words might appear in the empty spaces.

Two more examples of how prediction works:

- Nouns are predicted by articles and adjectives:
  the dog, *a* rat, *great* poet

- A verb is predicted by the appearance of a subject:
  A woman _____ us that she _____ that job.

More on prediction later.

Now I will discuss a significant method of gaining control over the sentence—*chunking*. Many of the longer messages shoved from left to right through the narrow space of the sentence should be chunked—broken up into readable units—so that the reader can process the information. As a result of chunking, you create a sentence unit which can be a single word, phrase, clause, or a recognizable cluster of these.

For some reason, many of us tend to write long sentence units that the reader has trouble processing:

> There have been no flu deaths from even the most viru-
> lent types of the disease for the past ten years in the
> county.

If you break that sentence into smaller chunks, the reader can process it more easily (note punctuation, which shows where chunks start and stop):

> For the past ten years **,** there have been no flu deaths in
> the county —— not even from the most virulent
> types of the disease.

In the act of chunking, you create recognizable units and separate them with punctuation marks:

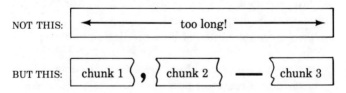

Observe that the issue is not just one of sentence length, although length has something to do with a readable style. The more readable of the two sentences on flu deaths is actually one word longer than the less readable. More important, usually, is the length and clarity of the chunk, which should be kept short and perfectly "fitted" to its idea. That is, the form and the content of the chunk should mesh.

Using only our simple diagram, typical chunked sentences will look like these *(note the punctuation marks, which show the break between chunks):*

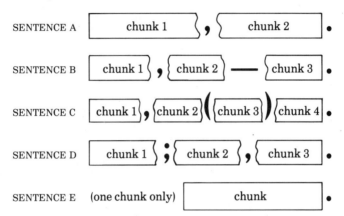

Examine the following examples of chunking using real words. Note, again, how the punctuation marks separate the chunks.

EXAMPLES OF CHUNKING

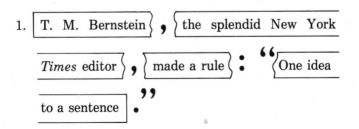

2. Applying this rule , said Bernstein , was one way of " achieving clarity and swift comprehension . "

3. But Bernstein's rule was not a formula to be applied thoughtlessly .

4. If you keep sentences reasonably short , they will probably be clear .

5. But more important for readability , perhaps , is this notion : As you feed your reader ideas , make them bite-sized — one chunk at a time .

6. Just don't try to jam too many ideas into one chunk ; you'll give your reader a stomach-ache .

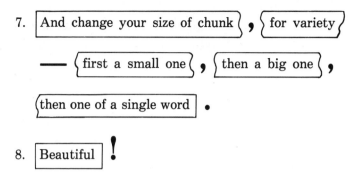

7.   And change your size of chunk , for variety

    —— first a small one , then a big one ,

    then one of a single word .

8.   Beautiful !

Let's pause here for a minute to consider what we have said about the sentence. First, from the reader's point of view: The reader starts on the left of the page and sweeps rightward at high speed—say, 300 to 400 words a minute. He is confined to the narrow space of the sentence as surely as if he were a locomotive moving swiftly on its tracks. And derailing a reader is a lot easier than derailing a train.

As your reader sweeps along the sentence, he processes your ideas in chunks, small units of meaning often separated by punctuation. If you give him too large a chunk or too many chunks at once, he may be derailed.

In addition, you make this whole operation work more smoothly by making sentences as predictable as possible—within reason, of course. Complete predictability would be miserably boring, a matter we will return to.

Now for your point of view as the writer: You travel through the sentence, just ahead of your reader. You watch him closely to see that he is on track. If he is about to get into trouble, you consider stopping to make repairs in the sentence.

Our next topic is building and repairing the sentence. The "rules" I suggest for doing this vary a good deal in generality, type, and application. They have perhaps only one thing in common: They have helped many writers I know.

RULE ONE: Every day, read some good writing: fiction, poetry, drama, essays, speeches.

Writing sentences is an art. Like any other art, it is full of strategy and technique. But it is also full of mystery and wonder, which do not take kindly to being chopped up and then scrunched down under numbered rules. You need to gain a feel for stylish sentences: for the weight, shape, sound, and taste of them.

I read somewhere that Henry Luce hired poets to write on business subjects in *Fortune* on the theory that they could be taught economics easier than economists could be taught writing. Whether the story is true or not, it ought to be.

RULE TWO: Use genuinely familiar words.

This replaces the old rule that said "Use short words." The length of a word is less important than its genuine familiarity. Why *genuine?* Many words, particularly those presently in vogue or in some way faddish, are familiar more as noises than as representations of exact meaning. When *detente* was in every headline, I asked many educated people what it meant. Almost no one knew. Later I asked ten people who worked professionally with language what the familiar term *passive voice* meant. The only person who came close was my secretary. On thousands of highway signs you'll find the expression *trauma center.* I asked twenty educated Americans what that meant, and no one knew for certain, although four made good guesses.

The genuinely familiar word is often homely and plain. The finest geophysicist I worked with (back when I was an engineer) often used the words *high* and *low* instead of *anticline* and *syncline*. His reports were wonderfully readable and the envy of other engineers. Of course he also had good ideas, without which the best words are useless.

RULE THREE: Keep on chunking.

Break sentences into clearly defined chunks, separated by punctuation. Examine this extended example of chunking:

(1) Police had arrested Chadwick and his companions at a Boston train station for possession of marijuana. (2) After incarcerating the suspects at the federal building, the police searched a footlocker which Chadwick had been carrying. (3) Significantly, the search—which occurred at the federal building—was conducted one and one-half hours after the arrest. (4) The police did not have a warrant allowing the search. (5) At his trial, Chadwick challenged the admissibility (into evidence) of the marijuana found in the footlocker, claiming that the search violated the fourth amendment.—written by a young lawyer.

Here you have *five* sentences broken into *eleven* chunks. There is no magic ratio, of course, between sentences and chunks. Nor is there any firm rule about where chunks should be placed in the sentence. But we do know that punctuated chunks at the beginning of the sentence—see (2), (3), and (5) above—are of particular value. The writer needs them to help prepare readers for ideas coming up, and to create necessary transitions. A style with too few of these "sentence beginners" will not read easily.

RULE FOUR: Use sentence signals to predict ideas.

Signals are words like *since, because, while, when, but, and, so, before.* For good predictability, they should be placed early in the sentence, either as the first word in the opening unit or as a word coming just before the main clause:

> *Because* he likes pickles, he bought two jars.

> *But* the president changed her mind.

When signals appear later in the sentence, as they sometimes do, they are designed to enhance the reader's predictions:

> Napoleon loved only himself, *but unlike* Hitler he hated nobody.—J. C. Herald

RULE FIVE: Make your subjects and verbs absolutely clear.

Typically, unreadable sentences begin to be unreadable on the left, in the crucial subject. Start wrong, and you will end wrong:

> Functional *microspace* implies the . . .

> *Symptomatology* relative to . . . manifests . . .

> A conceptual *relationship* as a means to an end is . . .

If you combine a poor choice of subject with a poor choice of verb, the sentence will just lie there comatose, perhaps dead:

> Behavior *problems act out* their relationships. (A *problem* can't *act out.*)

> *Isolation stigmatizes* the individual. (*Isolation* can't *stigmatize.*)

Writers and editors are forever tinkering with the subject and verb of sentences in order to make them more readable:

BAD: The government's *investigation* into the shipment of wheat by the exporter *was met* by his refusal in regard to an examination of his method of payments for its domestic transportation.

BETTER: The *government investigated* the shipment of wheat by the exporter. . . . But *he blocked* the investigation by refusing to . . .

BAD: The *causes* of the mutation of the genes *received* analysis from the scientists.*

BETTER: The *scientists analyzed* the causes of the mutation of the genes.

RULE SIX: Use parallel structures forcefully.

Parallelism refers to a listing of sentence elements which are (a) roughly equal in importance or emphasis, and (b) written in the same form. Parallel items can be anything from single words to full sentences.

SHORT ITEMS:

rod and reel

rod, reel, and bait

I need a rod, I need a reel, and I must have some bait.

RELATIVELY LONG ITEMS:

a new steel rod and a rusty old reel

a new steel rod, a rusty old reel, and fresh wriggling bait

---

*I borrowed the bad sentences from examples provided by Professor Joseph Williams in *Style: Ten Lessons in Clarity and Grace.* The rewrites are mine.

I need a new steel rod with plenty of flexibility, I would like to replace the rusty old reel, and I want the best possible bait for trout fishing in cool weather.

Parallelism allows you to state ideas *quickly* and *economically* (the italicized words are their own example). In addition, it gives your prose a pleasant strength and musical rhythm. Many memorable sentences depend on the balancing that parallelism encourages:

{Four score and seven} years ago our fathers brought forth upon this continent a new nation, {conceived in liberty and dedicated to the proposition} that all men are created equal.—Abraham Lincoln

The Lord is {my strength and my shield}.—Bible, King James Version

A sudden violent jolt of corn likker has been known to {stop the victim's watch, snap his suspenders, and crack his glass eye right across}.—Irvin S. Cobb

We hold these truths to be self evident: {that all men are created equal; that they are endowed by their creator with certain unalienable rights}; that among these are {life, liberty, and the pursuit of happiness}.... —Thomas Jefferson

{The energy, the faith, the devotion} which we bring to this endeavor will light {our country and all who serve it}—and the glow from that fire can truly light the world.—John F. Kennedy

Professors have told me I stress parallelism too much. But it is difficult to overstress parallelism because it is one of the fundamental structures in English, a part of the "masonry of syntax," as Sheridan Baker called it. In her computer study of parallelisms, Mary Hiatt discovered that more than 50 percent of the sentences in her large sample employed them—rather more than 50 percent, probably; her computer could not be programmed to catch them all.

Any experienced editor will tell you that a lot of poor prose occurs when a writer's unconscious mind tries to make things parallel but the conscious mind won't cooperate:

POOR: Also predominant on a boy's mind during his high school years are the desire for sexual activity, the want for a car, experimenting with smoking and drinking, and the testing of authority.

BETTER: During high school some boys can think only of {smoking, drinking, sex, and rebellion}.

POOR: The church group voted on invitations to senior citizens to meetings, decided why there was a necessity for the formation of a Senior Committee, and a Senior Sunday.

BETTER: The group decided {to form a Senior Committee and to establish a Senior Sunday}. They also voted to invite seniors to meetings. (two sentences)

Sometimes you will have to back up to the left of a sentence in order to make it more predictable *and* parallel:

POOR: The quality of a comic strip exists in relation to the drawings, the language as well as the situations involved.

The problem begins on the left with the subject and verb. What can the reader make of *quality exists?* Having stumbled over these words of his own, the writer fell flat, and so did the reader. So we fix the left part of the sentence and nail down the parallelism:

A comic strip is only as good as its *drawings, language,* and *situations.*

RULE SEVEN: Treat nouns, particularly abstract ones, as creatures of the devil.

Unless the construction is familiar and idiomatic, don't modify nouns with nouns. These are bad:

ramification potentials
resource use
attitude myopia

Another indication of noun disease (the phrase illustrates its own condition) is a trail of prepositions:

English teachers agree that personal ownership and use *of* a good dictionary is a prime necessity *for* every student *in* obtaining the maximum results *from* the study *of* English.

We can edit this by cutting some nouns and altering others. In the edited sentence we have reduced the prepositions from five to none, the nouns from ten to three:

English teachers agree that students should own and use a good desk dictionary.

RULE EIGHT: Where possible, use *who does what* and *what does what.*

If a sentence goes bad on you, ask it: Who is doing what here? (Just as useful, sometimes: What *is* what here?) And keep asking until the sentence gives you an answer.

BAD: Accordingly, there is a tremendous emphasis on PE and recreation beginning in the junior high which accounts for the significant increase in the accident rate for grades 7 through 12.

BETTER: (after three rewrites): Beginning in junior high, schools emphasize PE and recreation for the first time. For example, about 40 percent more students play touch football, softball, and soccer. So, starting in grade 7, the accident rate in school increases.

RULE NINE: Surprise your reader once in a while.

Don't always be serious or predictable. This anti-principle seems to apply to life generally; we all want variety. No person is interesting unless he or she surprises occasionally.

Immediate readability is not always a virtue. Clarity can be tiresome and plebeian. In an odd way, it can even militate against understanding an idea. If you want to know more about leadership, for instance, it may be a mistake to read one of the hundred straight-forward textbook discussions of the subject. Perhaps it would be better to read the works of an unpredictable genius—the tactics of Lord Nelson, the speeches of Churchill, the messages of Abraham Lincoln to his generals. Lincoln telegraphed to General McClellan: "I have just read your despatch about sore-tongued and fatigued horses. Will you pardon me for asking what the horses of your army have done since the battle of Antietam that fatigues anything?"

The more genuinely and permanently readable a writer, the more likely he is to surprise you. Here are a few lines from a recent essay, "Reading, Writing, and Typing," by John Kenneth Galbraith:

> All professions have their own way of justifying laziness. Harvard professors are deeply impressed by the jeweled fragility of their minds. More than the thinnest metal, these are subject terribly to fatigue. More than six hours of teaching a week is fatal—and an impairment of academic freedom. . . .
>
> Richly evocative and deeply percipient theory I avoid. It leaves me cold unless I am the author of it. . . .
>
> In the case of economics there are no important propositions that cannot be stated in plain language. . . .
>
> *(Concluding paragraph)* You might say that all this constitutes a meager yield for a lifetime of writing. Or that writing on economics, as someone once said of Kerouac's prose, is not writing but typing. True.

Galbraith keeps his reader slightly, delightfully, off-balance. From sentence to sentence, he changes the pattern of the main clause, using many of the available patterns in English:

All professions have their own way . . .	Subject-verb-object
Harvard professors are deeply impressed . . .	Subject-passive verb
More than six hours of teaching is fatal . . .	Subject is adjective
There are no important propositions . . .	Delayed subject—*propositions*
Writing on economics . . . is not writing but typing . . .	Subject is verbal noun

Galbraith also shifts the rhetoric of his sentences, jumping from normal order:

these are subject terribly to fatigue

to inverted order:

Richly evocative and deeply percipient theory I avoid.

to a one-word fragment at the end:

True.

And the reader is tantalized with the unexpected. Professions justify *laziness?* Harvard professors have minds of *jeweled fragility?* The metaphor darts and stings. He extends its theme into a metaphorical modulation and then drops into burlesque created by a parallelism: "More than six hours of teaching a week is fatal—and an impairment of academic freedom."

Galbraith is readable for all the reasons suggested by the authorities on rhetoric, from Aristotle on. But as important as any of these reasons is his gift of surprise mixed with blandishment. Partly we *want* to read him because we are never sure what he is going to do next.

RULE TEN: "Break any of these rules sooner than say anything outright barbarous."

Thus wrote George Orwell in his famous essay, "Politics and the English Language." You can not only break the rules, but modify and add to them. They are only suggestions after all.

It is appropriate to end with a few interesting sentences, taken from three hundred years of English prose.

I have never been in love. Sometimes the tears start to my eyes, but they never fall.—letter from Arnold Bennett to H. G. Wells

I cannot see on what grounds the king of Britain can look up to heaven for help against us; a common murderer, a highwayman, or a housebreaker, has as good a pretence as he.—Tom Paine

There is a hard pathos about Thoreau, the wanness of a stripped unblossoming tree against a gray sky. He was intellectually one of the bravest men that ever lived, and also a clammy prig.—Ludwig Lewisohn

He liked short paragraphs, hated long sentences, and never used a semicolon in his life.—James Thurber

Seven years, my Lord, have now passed, since I waited in your outward rooms, or was repulsed from your door, during which time I have been pushing on my work through difficulties of which it is useless to complain, and have brought it, at last, to the verge of publication, without one act of assistance, one word of encouragement, or one smile of favor. Such treatment I did not expect, for I never had a patron before.—Samuel Johnson.

All animals are equal, but some animals are more equal than others.—George Orwell

Continue until the tanks stop, then get out and walk.—General Patton, when informed of a shortage of tank fuel

Among those whom I like or admire, I can find no common denominator, but among those whom I love, I can: all of them make me laugh.—W. H. Auden

Capitalism is a failure, socialism is a failure, the welfare state has failed—but martinis *never* fail.—sign on barroom wall

I had not known my father very well. We had got on badly, partly because we shared, in our different fashions, the vice of stubborn pride. When he was dead I realized that I had hardly ever spoken to him. When he had been dead a long time I began to wish I had. It seems to be typical of life in America, where opportunities, real and fancied, are thicker than anywhere else on the globe, that the second generation has no time to talk to the first.—James Baldwin

If you haven't got common sense, the best thing to do is not get out of bed in the morning.—Harry Truman

O eloquent, just, and mighty death!—Sir Walter Raleigh

CHAPTER 7

EXPLAIN, EXPLAIN

Writing is designed to provide explanations. They make your reader happy he spent his time with you instead of reading novels or drinking martinis. The reader wants to know; and you explain by giving specific details, examples, particulars.

Readers are always curious. If you tell them that Americans are no longer safe—any of us—from crime, they will probably be bothered by this easy generalization and curious about how you intend to support it. Hodding Carter II explained it by a recitation of specific events:

Crime Epidemic: "It Can't Happen to Me"

To which I can only reply "Sez you." While it is said to be unwise to make sweeping generalizations based upon limited data, the following occurrences have everything to do with my attitude. They happened over a five-year period:

In early 1977, professional burglars kicked in the back door of our home in Alexandria, Va., and made a leisurely sweep of the premises. They cleaned out most of my wife's jewelry and took a gold watch which had been passed down from William Hodding Carter to William Hodding Carter for four generations. It is probable that they didn't take the kitchen sink as well only because one of our children returned while the burglary was in progress and scared them away. It was just lucky, the police said, that they were pros. Amateurs might have been rattled by the interruption and hurt her badly.

Not long thereafter, my fiercely independent mother was mugged while trying to find a taxi outside the East Side Airline Terminal building in New York, having just arrived from her home in Mississippi. The mugger knocked her down and ran off with her purse. Luckily, she was only shaken up.

About the same time, my brother's apartment in Mississippi was burglarized twice. Virtually everything of value was carted off.

Early last year, my 20-year-old daughter was returning to her apartment in New Orleans when two men made a lunge at her on the sidewalk. She sprinted away, made it through the front door and slammed it shut just ahead of her pursuers. That night she called and asked whether I thought she should carry a small pistol for self-protection. (I said no, but wrestled a little with the answer. The delayed response from this long-time gun-control advocate was instructive.)

Over the past two years, thieves and burglars have plundered our oldest son's car, parked behind his downtown Washington apartment, several times, and broken into the building as well. Just a few months ago, during a brief period when my car was parked in a garage in Midtown Manhattan, someone neatly punched open the locked trunk and stole several suitcases. Nobody saw it happen.

And, on a minor but somehow appropriate note, there was the Pawley's Island Hammock, a gift from old friends in North Carolina, which hung in the backyard of our summer place in Camden, Maine. On the next to last night of an otherwise idyllic vacation, someone sneaked it away. He went to infinite trouble to do so and risked discovery in the course of a crime whose object was of far more sentimental value to its owners than it could ever be of financial value to the thief.

Writing that is too general does not explain sufficiently:

I learned very quickly last summer that there was one thing you had to understand immediately when you worked around a waterhole drilling rig: safety was the watchword. Rigs are dangerous. I had to be careful and watch my step. One of the other roustabouts forgot this, and he got badly hurt.

The reader wonders what this is all about—why was "safety" the "watchword"? Why was a drilling rig "dangerous"? How and why did another roustabout get hurt? Here is the passage rewritten—to explain. The writer's explanatory material is italicized.

During operation, a *drilling rig* is dangerous at *three times:* when the *head driller* is *breaking out, putting pipe on,* or *drilling hard.* Take *breaking out (removing pipe),* for instance. The driller *signals* when he wants his *helper* to put his *wrench* on the *pipe.* When he is ready, he will *clutch-out* and throw the *rotary table* into *reverse.* After the table begins to turn, if the helper does not take his *hand* off the wrench he will get his *fingers cut off* because the wrench *slams* against the *drilling mast* with the force of *200 horsepower* behind it. One roustabout, *Billy Lawe,* got careless one day and lost *three fingers* on his *left hand.*

As a writer, you cannot create reality. You can only create its best substitute by supplying generalities and their supporting details. Your reader needs them both.

Imagine how empty and unconvincing this description of Theodore Roosevelt would be without its explanatory details:

> When referring to Theodore Roosevelt I do not use the word "giant" loosely. "Every inch of him," said William Allen White, "was over-engined." Lyman Gage likened him, mentally and physically, to two strong men combined; Gifford Pinchot said that his normal appetite was enough for four people. Charles J. Bonaparte estimated that his mind moved ten times faster than average, and TR himself, not wanting to get into double figures, modestly remarked, "I have enjoyed as much of life as any nine men I know." John Morley made a famous comparison in 1904 between Theodore Roosevelt and the Niagara Falls, "both great wonders of nature." John Burroughs wrote that TR's mere proximity made him nervous. "There was always something imminent about him, like an avalanche that the sound of your voice might loosen." Ida Tarbell, sitting next to him at a musicale, had a sudden hallucination that the President was about to burst. "I felt his clothes might not contain him, he was so steamed up, so ready to go, to attack anything, anywhere."—Edmund Morris

All kinds of writing, including those that are scientific or technical, require specifics to help them explain. Here is an engineer, discussing one aspect of *seismic migration* in geophysics. I have italicized the explanatory specifics in the passage:

> This *three-dimensional* migration points up certain aspects of *seismic lines.* One is the *curved line.* A seismic line is laid out as a *straight line* if at all possible, so the data *will stack* properly. However, there are occasions when a line must *curve* or not be *shot* at all. Examples are *marine-type shooting in a river,* which must follow the

river's course, and *land shooting in a narrow and winding valley.* These curved lines constitute a very special situation when there is also *steep dip* in the area.—J. A. Coffeen

Years ago, I had a teacher who used to remark regularly in class: "Don't tell me, *show* me! When she thought we students weren't supplying enough details and examples in our papers, she would write a large red SHOW!! in the margin. It was a good lesson. She taught us to respect the reader's interests. And also to respect the writer's time-honored purpose: to encourage belief and action through the use of specific explanation.

THE GLAMOUR
OF GRAMMAR

A LITTLE HANDBOOK OF SUGGESTIONS
AND DESPERATE REMEDIES

INTRODUCTION

ON THE TRAIL OF THE FEROCIOUS *NONE-ARE*

About grammar there are two ideas you should not believe. One is that grammar matters enormously. The other is that it does not matter at all.

The truth is somewhere in between. More precisely, there are many "truths" about grammar, some of which aren't very true. For example, my wife and I started a grammatical ruckus by using the expression *none are* in a letter to *The Wall Street Journal.* Readers of the *Journal* liked the letter, and by the dozen wrote and phoned to tell us so. There was even a letter from Japan. But most of our correspondents sadly noted our use of *none are:* "It should be *none is.*" One anonymous correspondent ascended to satire: "Nobody are perfect."

True. But on that occasion we were perfect about *none are.* Good writers have employed the usage for hundreds of years, and authorities have accepted it for at least a century. *Moral:* Don't tell someone he makes errors in grammar unless you know they are errors.

It is also helpful to understand what sort of beast you have cornered when you find a long-tailed, furry *None-are* cowering behind the furnace in the basement and showing its teeth. Is it a bad sort of beast? Will it bite? Should you call the cops, the humane society, or the Grammar Hotline?

I recommend that you call the nearest bookstore and ask if they have any of the usage books listed on page 72. And try the library, which is sure to have one or more of them. In Evans and Evans, for instance, you will discover that *none* has been used as a plural for a long time and that it "is always treated as a plural when it refers to persons." So you can give your beast in the basement some warm milk and an old rug to sleep on, in the calm confidence that its ancestors were housebroken by at least Shakespeare's time.

None are is one of the thousands of "grammatical" points that we really ought to consider as questions of *usage.* A purely grammatical question involves mainly the structure or basic coding system of the language. You would not say "The cat are" because the grammatical code does not allow it. *Grammar* tends to be obligatory, like the *what* in "I wonder what she is doing today."

By contrast, questions of *usage* tend to be less obligatory and more debatable, like *none are. None* looks like a singular and can act like one, as in "None of the work was done on time." As you can see, *none* tends to be singular or plural, depending on whether the idea in the sentence is singular or plural.

Usage also covers a great many linguistic problems that can't be easily explained by grammatical analysis.

The largest class of these, perhaps, is idioms. Idioms are expressions like *put up with* (for *tolerate*) and *walk back and forth*. You can't say *walk forth and back*, although you ought to could—an idiom I just remembered from childhood.

The foregoing discussion should make you feel better and give you confidence. Because the point of it all is that as a reasonably well educated native speaker of English, you will make relatively few errors in *grammar*. You will make some in *usage* when you are faced with competing choices in structure and wording.

So what should you do? Here is some advice.

First, relax. You are a normal user of English, but you won't write normally if you are tied in knots.

Second, go back and look at the material in Chapter Six, particularly the material on *chunking* (pages 46–49 and 51) and Rules 3 through 8. I've been experimenting with these rules for years with many kinds of writers. The evidence shows that if a writer will learn the rules *cold*, and practice their preachments, something remarkable happens. His writing becomes easier to do. It becomes clearer. He knows where he is in a sentence and why. Also, the number of so-called grammatical errors diminish, often spectacularly. Why? Because many errors are caused by the writer's sense of desperation as he wrestles with that slippery snake, the English sentence. Once he realizes that the snake is harmless, he has better control over it.

A third piece of advice concerns the astonishing number of imperfections built into English. Everywhere you look you find flaws and inconsistencies in the language itself. We should feel no surprise at this. Language is a human invention, and we humans are far from perfect.

My suggestion, then, is—Don't fight the imperfections. For that matter, consider not fighting any construction in English that gives you trouble as you write. When a pothole appears before you as you drive anxiously through a sentence, stop. Why crash into the pothole? Why not drive around it—avoid it?

An *avoidance* is not a cop-out, but a valid way around a linguistic problem. Instead of confronting the problem and attempting to solve it with a standard solution, you avoid it by using a different construction. In this way, you are not locked into a fixed response to a problem. Your writing can take on a new flexibility if you recognize that you have choices other than the standard solutions. As an example, consider the familiar problem of agreement with *either-or* and *neither-nor*. It is not hard to remember that with singular nouns in the subject, these pairs take singular verbs. You simply memorize this fact and apply it when necessary:

Neither the car *nor* the truck *was* stolen.

But what do you use when there is one car and two trucks?

Neither the car *nor* the trucks *was* (?) *were* stolen.

Neither *was* nor *were* sounds right, although the usage rule says that *were* is the proper choice—"the verb should agree with the nearer of its subjects."

It is often possible to avoid such a problem (and the possibility of error) by using one of several different constructions that will say pretty much the same thing. Here are a few:

PROBLEM: Neither the car nor the trucks *was*(?) *were*(?) stolen.

AVOIDANCES: The car *was* not stolen. Neither *were* the trucks.
The trucks *were* not stolen. Nor *was* the car.
The trucks and the car *were* not stolen.
The car and the trucks *were* still there.
The car *was* not stolen, and the trucks *weren't* either.
The trucks and the car *have not been* stolen.
The thieves *left* the car and the trucks.

It is difficult to talk about grammar, more difficult than doing it. Grammatical theory is like an angry porcupine, all motion and sharp points. Wherever you grab it, you wish you had grabbed it somewhere else. But *doing* grammar is not so painful, once you realize that the basic grammatical operations are as normal as breathing and that millions of English speakers perform the operations every day.

And perhaps it will lessen the pain to recall that the words *glamour* and *grammar* have common historical roots. As John Ciardi notes in his fascinating *Browser's Dictionary, glamour* once meant "the art of contriving magic spells," and *magister glomerie* meant "a master of grammar (of learning), the title of a medieval master of Cambridge University."

In modern times, *glamour* and *grammar* both have their magic and witchery. Indeed one suspects many a grammarian of using witchcraft on us poor folk, and of trying to subdue us through language spells no more real or effective than bats' wings dissolved in boiling water. Aroint thee, grammatical witch! Clear off—and take your potions, hexes, and *none is-es* with you. Don't call us; we'll call you.

SOME HELPFUL BOOKS ON GRAMMAR AND USAGE

Bernstein, Theodore, *The Careful Writer: A Modern Guide to English Usage.* New York: Atheneum, 1965.

_____, *Do's, Don'ts and Maybes of English Usage.* New York: New York Times Books, 1977.

Ebbitt, Wilma R. and David R. Ebbitt, *Writer's Guide and Index to English,* 7th ed. Glenview, Ill.: Scott, Foresman, 1982.

Evans, Bergen and Cornelia Evans, *A Dictionary of Contemporary American Usage.* New York: Random House, 1957.

Follett, Wilson, *Modern American Usage.* New York: Hill and Wang, 1966.

Fowler, H. W., *Modern English Usage,* 2nd ed. London: Oxford University Press, 1965.

Morris, William and Mary Morris, *Harper Dictionary of Contemporary Usage.* New York: Harper and Row, 1975.

THE GRAMMAR OF STATEMENTS

You have four major ways to make statements in sentence form:

1. Something does [something]. (shows *action*)

    Jane shoots John.

    Jane ran away.

    John should not have irritated her.

2. Something is [something]. (shows *is*-ness or *state of being*)

Jane is a good shot.

Jane's action will seem hasty.

John might have been less obnoxious.

The verb most often used here is a form of *be—was, am, is, were, been, are.* You can also use *seem, appear, become, taste, feel.*

3. Something is done [by something]. (the so-called *passive* construction)
   This statement is the reverse of 1 above:

   John was shot by Jane.

   Jane will be hunted by the police.

   Jane may be irritated by John again when he gets out of the hospital.

4. It (there) is something.

   There will be a shooting.

   It's a good day for revenge.

   There was no telling what Jane might do when provoked.

In ordinary writing, you will use statements 1 and 2 most of the time—when you are writing efficiently. Most of the ideas you try to express will fit these statement patterns easily. By the way, the popular notion that forms of *be* are colorless or inefficient is ludicrously wrong. Just try to describe or identify anything while avoiding *is, were, are,* etc. Indeed, by computer count, *is* is the most-used verb in standard edited English.

Use statements 3 and 4 sparingly. But they do have their value. Number 3 (the *passive*) is good for variety, and for making certain kinds of explanation:

The valve was removed by the plumber, who has left for the day.

And for those times you don't know who "did it":

This valve has been removed!

The *it (there)* statement is good for beginnings:

There are at least ten ways to act the part of Hamlet.

For stating conditions or values:

It's a beautiful day.

For giving a judgment:

There's no business like show business.

CORRECTING GRAMMATICAL ERRORS

NOUNS

MISUSE OF POSSESSIVE WITH -ING *NOUN*

An *-ing noun* is a naming word that ends in *-ing:*

Pitching is fun.

Learning is hard.

His *drinking* is hard to take.

When the emphasis is on the *activity,* use the *possessive* form with the *-ing noun:*

PROBLEM: She did not object to me *hugging* her.

SOLUTION: She did not object to *my hugging* her.

PROBLEM: The *officer commanding* me to pull over was a surprise.

SOLUTION: The *officer's commanding* me to pull over was a surprise.

If the emphasis is not on the activity, you may write:

She did not object to *me* hugging her. (But she might have objected to any other person who hugged her.)

I prefer *John* pitching. (The emphasis is on John, rather than on his activity, pitching.)

WRONG FORM OF PLURAL NOUN

Most nouns form the plural by adding *s* or *es: car/cars, person/persons, wish/wishes, rush/rushes.* If you are doubtful about a plural form, check your dictionary.

PRONOUNS

FAULTY PRONOUN AGREEMENT

Here is an example of faulty pronoun agreement: "*Everyone* was told to pick up *their* books and leave." Since *everyone* is singular, the pronoun *their* does not "agree" with it.

PROBLEM: I told *each woman* coming to the party to bring *their* own food.

SOLUTION: I told *each woman* coming to the party to bring *her* own food.

AVOIDANCE: I told *all the women* coming to the party to bring *their* own food. (Instead of forcing the pronoun to agree with the expression appearing earlier in the sentence, try starting the sentence with a more logical word. *Each woman* really means *all the women.*

Observe the typical choices in the following agreement problem:

PROBLEM: If you want *an employee* to work hard for you, always give *them* plenty of praise for good work.

SOLUTION: If you want *an employee* to work hard for you, always give *him* . . . .

AVOIDANCE: If you want *employees* to work hard for you, always give *them* . . . .

Note: Problems in pronoun agreement can often be avoided by going back to the beginning of the paragraph and deciding whether you want to be in the singular or the plural throughout your discussion. Decide early, for instance, whether you want to discuss *employees* in general, or the *employee* as an individual. Then simply be consistent in choosing pronouns.

For a comment on the "generic pronoun," see the Preface.

SHIFT IN PRONOUNS

As the note above suggests, you should plan ahead when choosing pronoun forms. Avoid inconsistencies like this:

PROBLEM: If traveling makes *one* sick, the airline provides paper bags for *you.*

SOLUTION (1): If traveling makes *one* sick, the airline provides paper bags for *him.*

(2): If traveling makes *you* sick, the airline provides paper bags for *you.*

(3): If traveling makes *people* sick, the airline provides paper bags for *them.*

AVOIDANCE: For anyone who gets sick, the airline provides a paper bag.

VAGUE PRONOUN REFERENCE

Make pronoun references clear:

PROBLEM: The dresser had glue blocks over the screw holes so that one had to remove the screws before removing the drawer supports. *This* required me to get help from my shop supervisor. (What does *this* refer to?)

SOLUTION: Since the dresser had glue blocks over the screw holes, I asked my shop supervisor to help me remove the blocks without damaging the drawer supports.

PROBLEM: Our dog knocked two lamps on the floor and broke several glasses on the lamp table. We found *them* smashed the next morning. (Does *them* refer to lamps, to glasses, or to lamps *and* glasses?)

SOLUTION: Our dog knocked .... We found the glasses smashed the next morning.

PROBLEM: In discussing the language requirements, *it* made us feel that we had the wrong idea about the usefulness of a foreign language. (What does *it* refer to?)

SOLUTION: As we were discussing the language requirements, we began to realize that we had the wrong idea about the usefulness of a foreign language.

WRONG FORM OF PRONOUN

To correct most errors in pronoun form, isolate (or set apart) the construction:

PROBLEM: Would you call Jack and *he* on the phone?

ISOLATION: Would you call *he?* (*He* should be *him.*)

SOLUTION: Would you call Jack and *him* on the phone?

PROBLEM: Phyllis and *me* will walk to the library with you.

ISOLATION: *Me* will walk to the library with you. (*Me* should be *I.*)

SOLUTION: Phyllis and *I* will walk to the library with you.

PROBLEM: The program was specially designed for *we* supervisors.

ISOLATION: The program was specially designed for *we.* (*We* should be *us.*)

SOLUTION: The program was specially designed for *us* supervisors.

The following advice is the subject of debate by many language experts. But it is practical advice and firmly based on modern English usage.

Who vs. *whom.* Use *whom* when it is the object of a preposition: "for whom," "to whom," "with whom." Use *who* with everything else.

I vs. *me; they* vs. *them;* etc. Where it sounds natural at the end of an expression, use the *object* form *(me, her, him, them)*:

It is *me.*

That is *them* over there.

This is *her* now.

ERROR IN AGREEMENT

Verbs must ordinarily agree with their subjects:

Dogs *are* popular pets.

The economist *was* Korean.

When in doubt, however, let your *meaning* determine the subject-verb agreement.

PROBLEM: A *number* of these cures *was*(?) *were*(?) rejected.

SOLUTION: A *number* of these cures *were* rejected. (Obviously, *number* designates more than one cure.)

AVOIDANCES: Several of these cures were rejected.

A few of these cures were rejected.

The doctors rejected some of the cures.

Here are some typical problems in agreement:

1. With clumsy joiners (*as well as, along with, in addition to,* etc.)

PROBLEM: My *baby,* together with three other babies in the maternity ward, *was*(?) *were*(?) saved by the nurse.

SOLUTION: My *baby,* together with three other babies in the maternity ward, *was* saved by the nurse. (The general rule is that a singular subject, immediately followed by clumsy joiners or other interrupters, takes a singular verb.)

AVOIDANCE: My *baby and* three other *babies* in the maternity ward *were* saved by the nurse. (Where you can, use *and* instead of clumsy joiners.)

2. With pronouns.

PROBLEM: She is one of those *women who is*(?) *are*(?) always well prepared.

SOLUTION: She is one of those *women who are* always well prepared. (Make the verb agree with the noun *[women]* that the pronoun *[who]* stands for.)

AVOIDANCE: She is the kind of *women who is* always well prepared. (Put the whole thing in the singular.)

3. With "subject-*is*-noun" statements.

PROBLEM: The main *issue is*(?) *are*(?) high prices.

SOLUTION: The main *issue is* high prices. (Make the verb agree with the subject.)

AVOIDANCE: The main *issue is* that *prices are* too high.

4. With collective nouns ("group" nouns).

PROBLEM: The *team is*(?) *are*(?) happy about their victory.

SOLUTION: The *team is* happy about its victory. (Consider the team as one group or unit.)

AVOIDANCE: The *members* of the team *are* happy about their victory. (Use a plural subject.)

PROBLEM: A *hundred feet* of electrical wire *is*(?) *are*(?) too much for this room.

SOLUTION: A *hundred feet* of electrical wire *is* too much for this room. (Consider a *hundred feet* as a unit.)

AVOIDANCE: We don't need a hundred feet of electrical wire for this room.

5. With "it-there" statements.

PROBLEM: *There is*(?) *are*(?) happy *cowboys* in Texas.

SOLUTION: *There are* happy *cowboys* in Texas. (Make the verb agree with the subject *cowboys*.)

AVOIDANCE: In Texas, some cowboys are happy.

ERROR IN TENSE

Usually this error occurs when you forget to continue in the verb "time" that you started with. Example:

PROBLEM: He *complained* loudly to the boss that *he is* tired.

SOLUTION: He *complained* loudly to the boss that *he was* tired.

Note: Use the present tense for plot summaries or comments about action in a narrative or dramatic work:

Othello *believes* that his wife *is* unfaithful.

Tom Sawyer *tricks* other boys into painting the fence for him.

SPLIT INFINITIVE

If an awkward construction is the result, do not "split" the *to* from its verb:

PROBLEM: *to* happily *find*

SOLUTION: *to find* happily

PROBLEM: I want you *to* rigorously *perform* your job.

SOLUTION: I want you *to perform* your job rigorously.

AVOIDANCES: I want you to perform your job as well as you can.

I want you to do an excellent job.

Please do a good job.

THE PROBLEM OF THE SUBJUNCTIVE

The subjunctive is a verb form used mainly in *contrary-to-fact* statements and after *wishes*. The verb form may be *were, be,* or the verb without the final *s*.

Contrary-to-fact statements:

I would not do that if I *were* you. (I am not you.)

If she *were* true to me she would not go out with other men. (She is not true to me.)

If this *be* patriotism, I am not a patriot. (This is not patriotism.)

After wishes:

I wish I *were* rich.

Let him *live*.

My father requested that his body *be* cremated.

I demand that Smith *be* reinstated. (A demand is a strong wish.)

ADJECTIVES AND ADVERBS

Problems with adjectives and adverbs are sometimes created when you confuse the two. For instance, if you wanted to say that someone had body odor, it would be silly to write that he smelled *badly*, for *badly* would imply that his nose wasn't working properly. Follow these suggestions for distinguishing between adjectives and adverbs:

1. Understand that adjectives modify nouns and that adverbs modify verbs, adjectives, and other adverbs.

2. Use your dictionary to check whether a word is an adjective or an adverb.

3. Substitute the word you are in doubt about into one of these patterns:

Subject-verb-*adjective*-object:

> You injured a *well* person.

> You did a *good* job.

Subject-verb-object-*adverb:*

> You did the job *well.*

> You did it *happily.*

Subject-is-*adjective:*

> It is *good.*

> She is *happy.*

The substitution should tell you whether the word is an adjective or adverb.

MODIFIERS

Modifiers are sentence elements that describe, qualify, or limit the meaning of an expression.

MISPLACED MODIFIERS

PROBLEM: I departed to Europe on a freighter three thousand miles away.

SOLUTION: I departed on a freighter for Europe—three thousand miles away.

SOLUTION: I got on a freighter bound for Europe, which was three thousand miles away.

PROBLEM: He nearly tried to make all of his children happy.

SOLUTION: He tried to make nearly all of his children happy.

PROBLEM: We discovered the old well in the north corner of Marston's back yard, which was full of green, brackish water. (The *yard* was full of water?)

SOLUTION: The old well that we discovered in the north corner of Marston's back yard was full of green, brackish water.

DANGLING MODIFIERS

Most dangling modifiers occur at the beginning of the sentence:

Having eaten his lunch, the steamboat departed.

Make sure that your opener modifes the subject of the following main clause:

Having eaten his lunch, he boarded the departing steamboat.

PROBLEM: Coming too fast to the stop sign, the brake was applied quickly.

SOLUTION: Coming too fast to the stop sign, the driver applied the brake quickly.

PROBLEM: Sitting down at the typewriter, the paper was written rapidly.

SOLUTION: Sitting down at the typewriter, I wrote the paper rapidly.

PROBLEM: Astonished at the intrusion, his hands fluttered wildly.

SOLUTION: Astonished at the intrusion, he fluttered his hands wildly.

AVOIDANCE: He was so astonished at the intrusion that he fluttered his hands wildly.

SENTENCE STRUCTURE

FALSE COORDINATION

To *coordinate* means to make grammatically equal. If you put "unequal" ideas into "equal" main clauses, you may create a false coordination:

PROBLEM: I had a lot of work to do, *and* I had a cup of coffee.

SOLUTION: Even though I had a lot of work to do, I had a cup of coffee.

PROBLEM: Liza was an excellent worker, *and* she got the best job in the company.

SOLUTION: Liza, *who was an excellent worker,* got the best job in the company.

FALSE COMPARISON

Here is an example of a false comparison: "Walcott's beliefs were different from Clark." The problem is that the writer is comparing the wrong things—*beliefs* and *Clark.*

SOLUTION (1):   Walcott's beliefs were different from Clark's.

SOLUTION (2):   Walcott's beliefs were different from those expressed by Clark.

FAULTY PARALLELISM

Parallel elements in a sentence should be (a) roughly equal in importance, and (b) written in the same grammatical form. Examples:

Roger and *Tom* were terrible at ballroom dancing.

Ballroom dancing and *square dancing* are not activities for sissies.

Some small nations preferred to *watch, listen,* and *wait* in order to see what the larger nations would do.

Faulty parallelism fails to put parallel *ideas* in parallel *form:*

PROBLEM: She *believes* in him, as well as *having* faith in him.

SOLUTION: She *believes* in him and *has* faith in him.

PROBLEM: That movie had too much *sex, violence,* and the *language was bad.*

SOLUTION: That movie had too much *sex, violence,* and *profanity.*

A FEW POINTS ON PUNCTUATION

1. USE A COMMA WHEN...

a. You join two main clauses with a coordinating conjunction (*and, or, but, so, for*):

The grass is bright green, *and* all the trees are beginning to bud.

The river is flooding, *but* Dad won't be there to see it.

It is extremely rainy here this season, *so* be sure to bring your raincoat when you come.

b. You join an opener, an interrupter, or a closer to a main clause:

Since Clarice was bored in the second grade, her parents decided to let her skip a grade.

We would not shake our pursuers, *although we tried to lose them several times that day.*

That's what I want to do, *join the Army.*

Our dachshund, *who was dozing near the fire,* suddenly began to bark loudly.

You grabbed my foot, *not my hand!*

c. You use a parallel construction of three or more elements:

griffins, dragons, and *elves*

Were there *green, yellow,* or *orange* colors in the painting?

This country must ban *arms, ammunition,* and *all other instruments of war.*

We lay on the ground, we stared at the stars, and *we thought deep thoughts.*

d. You place "equal" descriptive words before a noun:

new, nice-looking table

New and *nice-looking* describe *table,* a noun. They are "equal" because you can put *and* logically between them—"new *and* nice-looking." In the phrase "new coffee table," *new* and *coffee* are not equal: you wouldn't say "new *and* coffee table."

> *honest, wonderful* person (honest *and* wonderful person)
>
> *hot, dark* night (hot *and* dark night)
>
> But: *last spring* semester (not last *and* spring semester)

e. You employ direct address:

John, please wash the car.

Ms. Rosenthal, would you sit over there?

f. You supply dates and places:

Chicago, Illinois

January 15, 1984

On May 14, 1916, in Houston, Texas

He died in Nashville, Tennessee, on October 14, 1943.

g. You identify speakers in dialogue:

James said, "Where can I find my umbrella?"

"It's in the hall closet," I said.

"If that's the way you're faithful," said Marie angrily, "we're through!"

h. You want to prevent misreading or ambiguity:

> By speaking of the dead, Lincoln in his Gettysburg Address appealed to . . . .

If you write "By speaking of the dead Lincoln . . . " your reader may be confused and have to reread the sentence.

The deductions allowed, the taxpayer is able to . . . .

"The deductions allowed the taxpayer . . . " may be confusing.

2. USE A SEMICOLON WHEN . . .

   a. You want to join two main clauses without using a coordinating conjunction:

The snows of yesterday have all gone; they have melted away.

His technique on the guitar is sloppy; he doesn't seem to care whether he hits the right notes or not.

   b. You want to join two main clauses with "long" conjunctions (conjunctive adverbs) like *moreover, however, therefore, consequently:*

I caught you red-handed; *therefore,* you will go to jail.

Sam and Rena went to the church; *however,* they didn't get married.

The company cheated on its income tax; *consequently,* the Internal Revenue Service demanded back payment of tax.

Note: It is not necessary to discuss here the complicated theory of long conjunctions or conjunctive adverbs. Just remember that the *short* conjunction (*and, or, but, so,* etc.) between main clauses takes a comma, while the *long* conjunction takes a semicolon.

   c. You need to clarify a parallel series:

UNCLARIFIED: At the meeting were Smithers the captain, Jones the first mate, and Watterson the bosun.

CLARIFIED: At the meeting were Smithers, the captain; Jones, the first mate; and Watterson, the bosun.

UNCLARIFIED: My landlady tells my wife what kind of floor wax to use, the same as she uses, when to use it, the same time she does, where to set the refrigerator, the same place as hers, and, most helpful of all, when to get her husband up in the morning.

CLARIFIED: My landlady tells my wife what kind of floor wax to use, the same as she uses; when to use it, the same time she does; where to set the refrigerator, the same place as hers; and, most helpful of all, when to get her husband up in the morning.

3. USE A COLON WHEN...

a. You introduce a list:

Please buy the following: butter, cheese, and bread.

It is often simpler to omit the colon and write: "Please buy butter, cheese, and bread."

b. You introduce quotations:

Toward the end of his life, Smith wrote to his son, making this plea: "Whatever you decide to do with the old property as a whole, never sell the north woods, for they meant everything to your mother."

c. You punctuate the salutation in a business letter:

Dear President Winkleboom:
Dear Sir:

Dear Mr. Ryan:
Dear Ms. Perez:

4. USE PARENTHESES WHEN...

You wish to set off a word or an expression firmly from the rest of the sentence:

The man I am referring to (Jenkins) is not necessary to our plans.

There are not enough women doctors and lawyers (this is what the girl said).

When it was over the ship, the winch (which was holding up the boom) suddenly collapsed.

Parentheses *always* come in pairs. See *Note* below in 5.

5. USE A DASH WHEN...

You need to show a strong break in thought:

He became president only four years later—the youngest man ever in the post.

I never want to get married—not under any circumstances.

Is there—listen to me—is there any hope for the survivors?

Note: Parentheses and dashes are quite helpful when you want to clarify a sentence that is loaded with too many commas. Observe how this writer, having already used commas around one interrupter, chooses to employ dashes around a second:

Edward Cole, an engineer who owned one of the first 300 Corvettes produced in 1953, remembers that on his first long ride in the rain—from suburban Detroit 150 miles to Kalamazoo—the water rising in the cockpit compelled him to take off his shoes and roll up his pants.—Coles Phinizy, "The Marque of Zora"

Of course, the writer could have used parentheses around either one of his interrupters. Don't rely too heavily on parentheses or dashes.

6. USE AN APOSTROPHE WHEN...

a. You use a possessive form:

the *trailer's* wheel (one trailer)
The *trailers'* wheels (more than one trailer)
Peter's arm
Persius' style

Note: Do not use the apostrophe with personal pronouns: "*his* car," "these are *hers.*"

If you have trouble remembering whether the apostrophe goes inside or outside the *s,* simply think of this example. Take the word *dog,* add an apostrophe and the *s: dog's.* If the word already has an *s,* do the same—but drop the second *s.* And so *dogs* becomes *dog's* becomes *dogs'.* Here are a few additional examples:

"The water supply of the town" becomes "the *town's* water supply."

"The water supply of the towns" becomes "the *towns'* water supply."

"The house belonging to Roger" becomes "*Roger's* house."

"The house belonging to the Rogers family" becomes "the *Rogers'* house."

b. You form plurals using numbers or letters:

Last semester, she got three *A's,* two *B's,* and a *C.*

There are four *3's* in the winning lottery number.

The *1950's* were a time of relative peace in the world.

c. You form a contraction:

It's the thing to do.

He'll be there.

I *can't* be at home today.

7. USE A HYPHEN WHEN...

a. You need a syllable break at the end of a line:

real-ization   *stereo-phonic*   *incor-porate*

b. You use a prefix before a syllable starting with *e:*

pre-empt   *de-emphasize*   *re-enforce*

c. You make a compound word:

self-analysis   *cease-fire* (noun)   *mother-in-law*

d. You make a compound modifier:

a *one-year* clause   a *big-time* actor   a *blue-eyed* rabbit

When in doubt about the use of a hyphen, particularly for prefixes and syllable breaks, check your dictionary.

8. USE QUOTATION MARKS WHEN...

a. You quote the exact spoken or written words of somebody else.

"No country on earth," shouted Senator Blanksley, "is richer than ours!"

It was John Donne who first said that "no man is an island."

b. You refer to titles of television programs, songs, paintings, and short literary works:

Faulkner wrote the short story, "A Rose for Emily."

The song is called "Stardust."

Picasso's "Guernica" is one of the most famous paintings of the twentieth century.

"M*A*S*H" has always been my favorite television program.

9. USE ITALICS (UNDERLINING) WHEN...

a. You refer to specific words or phrases:

The word *fragrance* is euphonious.

I do not understand what Marx meant by *democracy*.

b. You emphasize a word or phrase:

Do the job *right.*

I was referring to John *Adams,* not John Addison.

c. You refer to the titles of novels, books, stage productions, magazines, and newspapers:

The Right Stuff (book)
Moby Dick (novel)
Hamlet (play)
La Traviata (opera)
The Sound of Music (movie)
Sports Illustrated (magazine)
St. Louis *Post-Dispatch* (newspaper)

The relative length of works determines whether you use quotation marks or italics. Faulkner's short story, "A Rose for Emily," is put in quotation marks, but his novels (like *Sanctuary*) are italicized. Milton's "L'Allegro" is a short poem; his *Paradise Lost* is long—interminable.

SIX SAMPLE WRITINGS FOR DISCUSSION

ONE

Once I had to write a brief account for an oil company magazine on the work done in the seismograph section. My audience ranged from lawyers to secretaries to chemists. I could use from 600 to 800 words.

I began by asking myself a few questions. What did my readers know about the topic? The chemists and some other technical people might know a little, perhaps, from their college training. But the others would know nothing. What would *all* my readers know? What would they have in common?

I made lists of common knowledge on scratch paper. (I use up a pad of yellow scratch paper almost every week.) Peering at the lists, I noticed two words: *earthquake* and *echo*. Everyone in my audience had some knowledge of these. In particular, everyone knew that sound travels at a certain rate in the air, and that echoes bounce off a surface.

Accordingly, I decided to use *echo* as a hook.

This hook immediately suggested an analogy. If I kept comparing sound echoes to seismic echoes, I could work from the familiar to the unfamiliar. Having settled on an organizational device, I started to write:

> The history of seismology is the history of trial and error. First, there are two types of instrumentation used, the refractive and reflective. The refractive, the earlier type . . . .

And stopped writing. This introduction got started in the wrong place and was threatening to go on forever. What had happened to my hook? Another question: As to organization, what should come first? Second? I reached for the scratch pad, on which I jotted this:

Hook: *echo*

1. sound waves and echo
2. ground waves and echo
3. interpreting the echo
4. weakness of analogy (?)
5. shut up

Number 5 reminded me to stop when I came to the end. Like many writers, I have trouble both starting *and* stopping. I jumped in:

1   You all know about the big seismographs that detect and measure earthquakes. The oil seismograph is a small portable electronic instrument that detects and measures artificial earthquakes. The purpose of the instrument is to find geological structures that may contain oil. Here is how it works.

2   Let me begin with an occurrence that should be familiar. Imagine yourself standing near the base of a large cliff. If you shout at the cliff face, you will get an echo because the sound waves bounce back from the so-

called "interface" where air meets rock. The sound waves travel at 1100 feet per second. You can find out how far you are standing from the cliff by measuring the time it takes for your shout to travel from you to the cliff and back again, and then by solving a simple formula for distance.

3   The function of the oil seismograph is to find out how far down in the earth the horizontal layers of rock are. To discover this distance, the oil seismologist digs a deep hole (usually 100–200 feet) in the surface of the ground. At the bottom of the hole, he explodes a heavy charge of dynamite. Ground waves travel from the explosion down to the layers of rock. At each major interface between the layers, the waves bounce back to the surface. The explosion is similar to shouting at the cliff. Just as sound travels through the air at a certain speed, ground waves travel through the earth, although much faster. Ground waves bounce from rock interfaces as sound waves bounce from a cliff face. And the seismologist can determine distance just as you can determine the distance between you and the cliff.

At this point, I thought of two things. First, I knew from experience that the description of the "deep hole" would cause trouble. Readers would ask: Why was it so deep—if we were only going to bury the dynamite just enough to keep the explosion from breaking windows and frightening livestock? The hole needed explanation.

Second, this piece was still going to run too long. After inspecting the scratch outline, I lined out number 3 and wrote a new note above it:

weathering and echo
3. ~~interpreting the echo~~

Then I went back to paragraph 3 and made an insertion:

To discover this distance, the oil seismologist digs a deep

hole (usually 100–200 feet) in the surface of the ground/
—the purpose of the hole I will

At the bottom of the hole . *explain later.*

The insertion told my reader to wait a minute, and I would explain the hole. Now we pick up paragraph 4—I already had my paragraph lead from what I imagined my reader's question would be:

4   Why does the seismologist dig a hole to explode the dynamite? Much of the ground surface is covered with what geologists call *weathering,* that relatively loose covering of soil, sand, clay, etc., that usually goes down to the water table. This weathering has a disastrous effect upon seismic waves in the ground; it slows them up and even disperses them. To explode a dynamite charge on top of the ground would be like shouting at a cliff face through a bowl of mush—no matter how loud you shouted, little of your voice would get through. So the seismologist drills through the weathering and plants the dynamite charge below it. Usually the weathering has a bad effect only on the waves at the point of explosion; the *reflected* waves will travel through the weathering to the instruments on the surface.

5   In the interest of accuracy, I should add that the analogy between air waves and seismic waves is partly literal and partly figurative. The principles are similar but the conditions are different. Air waves are relatively constant in speed because the medium varies little. Seismic waves, by contrast, increase in speed with depth, and the increase is irregular and difficult to measure. Also, seismic reflections vary in ways that no one completely understands. But the analogy is, in a basic sense, revealing and accurate enough to explain to you how an oil seismograph works.

Paragraph 4 is a series of *writer's answers-to-reader's-questions.* If you go back and read each sentence separately, you can see what I was trying to do—answer each question as it might pop into the reader's mind. First, I defined *weathering* right away. Then, when I mentioned the "disastrous effect" of weathering, I explained it with a metaphorical comparison using the bowl of mush. And so on.

In paragraph 5, I added a comment about the roughness of my analogy (and it is rough) and stopped typing.

A final observation. Read again the first sentence of each paragraph. I try to make these paragraph "leads" work hard. Sometimes they help to make a necessary transition. Often they provide a *promise:* "Here's where I'm going to lead you; follow me and you'll get there." Sometimes, in certain pieces of writing, it will take two or even three sentences to complete a paragraph promise. I prefer one sentence, but using more also works.

TWO

An editor asked me to write a short article on Nathanael West, specifically on his Hollywood novel, *The Day of the Locust.* I reread the novel, looked up the recent criticism, and planned the piece, which would run about 3,000 words.

Because I had some trouble getting a grip on the topic, I tried several hooks. Most of these I had to abandon early. I finally settled on a cluster of three hooks—one was *violence* in the novel; another was *causes* of violence. The third one I had trouble reducing to a word or phrase; you will see what I decided on in a minute.

When a piece of writing is intransigent or complex, I like to block out the action as if I were directing a play:

My "audience" should believe this: *Although West describes American violence believably in* The Day of the Locust, *he is weak at explaining its causes.*

Act I. Introduction
    A. Background
    B. Thesis stated

Act II. Characters and plot
    A. Description of characters
    B. Theme of frustrated love
    C. The violence of the riot

Act III. Types of violent scenes
    A. Sexual violence
    B. Mob violence

Act IV. The question of motivation and causes
    A. Violence out of proportion to cause
    B. Failure to connect cause to effect
    C. The questionable views of critics
    D. West as a surrealistic writer
    E. West's intellectual attitudes

Act V. Conclusion

Clearly, this is no more than a formal outline with a thesis written on the top. My hooks were *violence, weak,* and *causes.* I intended to hang the argument in the outline firmly on those hooks.

Here are the introduction and last two paragraphs of the essay. These are enough to show you how I shaped the drama of the argument—all writing (when it works) is *dramatic* in one or more senses of the word.

Note the promise (or thesis) of the last sentence in the introduction, and also how the thesis is picked up and echoed in the concluding paragraphs.

First Paragraph

Nathanael West's *The Day of the Locust* (published in 1939) is a novel about the people who live in Hollywood and the tourists who visit the area looking for excitement and a reason for living. Many of them, both tourists and residents, are bored and violent. Josephine Herbst wrote of the novel: "The finest passages are those in which violence, and particularly mob violence, is described and analyzed. . . ." Thus it would seem that *The Day of the Locust* would be an ideal work to use for an investigation of American violence, as it is presented in fiction. And so it is, with one important qualification. West *describes* violence beautifully, but his reader is often left wondering *why* the violence occurs as it does.

Last Two Paragraphs

If *The Day of the Locust* is surrealistic, then any questions about motivation may lack point. Yet a reader (this reader, anyway) gets the feeling that in presenting scenes of violence with such power and variety West was not merely giving us surrealistic drama sequences, but was also trying to tell us something. I sense in West certain attitudes toward life that he wished to express in rather traditional fictional forms, although he did not always use those forms. I am thinking of a remark made by an acquaintance of his, Robert M. Coates: "More than anyone else I've ever known, he was a fatalist, and a coolly pessimistic one at that." Josephine Herbst, who also knew him, referred to West's "nihilistic pessimism, the sense that all institutions are shams. . . ." These are intellectual, not surrealistic, attitudes; and they may help explain why a reader might find West's brilliant descriptions of violence lacking in motivation. Although he had ideas, his gift was for describing physical events in a surrealistic way, not for explaining those events. The surrealist is not generally interested in motivation anyway.

Whether or not the judgments on West's novel I have made are valid, I think it can be said that *The Day of the Locust* is a poor choice if one wants to find a work of fiction, like *The Grapes of Wrath*, that explains *why* men act as they do. *The Day of the Locust* shows, in almost endless detail, the terrors and violence of American life. But it does not, generally speaking, give reasons. For those, we shall have to look elsewhere.

Here are several rather different pieces of writing. As you read them, try working backwards to guess how the authors arranged and developed the ideas in them.

THREE

1   Doctors have been asked, all through their professional lives, when medical science will be able to do something about the common cold. It has long been taken as a standing rebuke to science in general that, for all the celebrated advances, from disposable razors to fusion reactors, we must still catch the grippe. But the technology is available, and now, I suppose, the time is near at hand when the cold can be conquered.

2   There will be something melancholy about this announcement, when and if it comes. There may be just time enough to do some fast second-thinking. Do we really want to be rid of the grippe?

3   These days we do not have many opportunities to become ill during the early years of life, and we do not understand, as we used to, this aspect of living. Young children do not, or need not, contract measles or

whooping cough or chicken pox. Scarlet fever is as much a thing of the past as are diphtheria, poliomyelitis, and typhoid fever. This is, of course, an unqualified good thing, saving many lives and sparing countless young people from protracted invalidism. All benefit, no question about it.

4 And yet, there is a certain kind of loss involved. Fifty years and more ago, children came to understand something important about the hazard of living and, more important, about mortality. It was a part of everyday experience, seen at first hand, part of growing up. The youngest child in the family down the block died of septicemia or meningitis. Another neighbor caught pneumonia and almost died. Schoolmates were kept home for months with rheumatic fever. Tuberculosis was the great risk to be feared, feared as cancer is today, and there was nothing to be done about it except worry.

5 For earlier generations in the last century, before living memory, typhoid was the thing to be frightened of every day. If you contracted typhoid you were caught up and swept along in a terrifying kind of game over which you had absolutely no control. If you went through this illness—six or eight weeks of rocketing fever and flat-out prostration, with the chance any day of having part of an intestine perforate or burst into hemorrhage—and you came out at the other end intact and well again, you knew you'd had a brush with death and had won a victory against high odds. Convalescence was a time for feeling pride. People who lived through lobar pneumonia—two weeks or so of glimpsing mortality each evening, then ending in what was called the "crisis," the sudden plummeting of the temperature within hours, and the sudden recovery— were entitled to a sense of triumph.

6 Very few people know about this side of life today, and they only learn it late in life. Serious illnesses tend to come along after middle age, and when they do strike, unexpectedly and catastrophically, they come as an outrage. For one who is not used to the idea of illness, it is a shocking, foreign experience, a violation of one's contract with life. Dying, which was once the most normal of events, always going on in someone's household around the corner, often enough in one's own, now takes place at a great distance, away in a hospital somewhere.

7 All to the good. But perhaps we can still do with periodic reminders of biological fallibility, in symbolic preparation for the real thing. This might be the contribution of the grippe to Western civilization, a kind of theatrical performance within the body, teaching, after the fashion of medieval stage plays, a kind of moral lesson: watch out.

8 The grippe will do. There is much to be said for a self-limited, never-fatal disability that takes one clean out of affairs for a few days, makes it impossible to work, allows one to take complainingly to bed. Under the right circumstances—surrounded by a family now obliged to display solicitude, comfortably propped on pillows with a thermometer in one's mouth reading an impressive 102 degrees, aching in all muscles, but with aspirin, codeine, maybe even good brandy coursing through one's veins—it can be an uplifting, heady experience.

9 I suggest that we leave the various viruses responsible for grippe off the list of diseases to be conquered, perhaps even place them somewhere on the roll of endangered species, to be welcomed into any home from time to time.

10 Doctors, especially young doctors and medical

students about to enter clinical training, are the most in need. Very few of today's medical school graduates have any idea what illness is like: They must try to learn about it second-hand, from books or lectures or by simply looking at sick people, which is a long way from real knowledge. It might be a good idea, once or twice in the academic year, to release an aerosol of grippe into the lecture hall during, say, the course in molecular biophysics. For advanced standing, students could volunteer to keep working through the days and nights of the illness, not taking to their beds at all, in order to catch the sense of what it is like *not* to be cared for, a useful kind of knowledge for any doctor.
—Lewis Thomas, "Getting a Grip on the Grippe"

FOUR

704 West Washington
Urbana, IL 61801

February 18, 1982

American Doozie Motor Company, Inc.
P.O. Box 70
Danda, CA 90247

ATTN: CUSTOMER SERVICE DEPARTMENT

SUBJECT: "Oh, the Oil Light Never Comes On Until It's Too Late!"

That's a direct quote from Twin City Doozie's service writer. She had just told me that it would cost me

$1400 to repair my 1981 Doozie (with 14,000 miles on it). When I asked why the oil light had never come on or why the car had never run hot to warn me the oil was low (in my case, nonexistent), that was her answer.

My questions to you: "What purpose do these supposed 'safeguards' serve? If they don't function until it's *too late,* why are we consumers cautioned to pay attention to them? And why should we have to pay for extras that don't work?"

Let me tell you our experiences so far with our 14,000-mile Doozie.

We bought it in April 1981—new, as an economy, around-town, second car. We faithfully had it serviced—according to your manual—at 5,000 miles, at 10,000 miles.

At approximately 13,000 miles, the clutch went out. The cable didn't break; the whole clutch assembly had to be replaced. I protested that I thought 13,000 miles too few to necessitate a complete clutch assembly. Evidently the dealer agreed; I was not billed for that $200.75.

At 13,822 miles, we were forced to replace the front tires—they were "slicks"—no doubt as a result of the faulty clutch. Again, 13,822 miles seemed far too soon for new tires, but I needed them, so we bought them—PLUS a new battery. Another $126.

Then the ultimate catastrophe. On December 9 (still 1,000 miles *before* our next scheduled service obligation), our son started to Springfield for a job interview in the Doozie (190-mile, round trip). Shortly before he reached the Buffalo exit, the oil light flashed—then immediately went out. He slowed, and when the oil light stayed off, resumed his journey. As he reached the Buffalo exit, the Doozie began to choke, cough, rattle, and knock—the oil light came on solid—and as he pulled off the road, the car died.

He was towed in by Anderson-Shell (2000 West Monroe, Springfield 62704), for $63.40. The servicemen who first examined the car said: "There is no oil in the engine. The 'white, sticky substance in the oil filter' is evidence of that. You'll need a complete engine overhaul." Yet we had followed your instructions to the letter; and no "oil light" or "temperature light" had ever warned us that we might be in trouble. We then had it towed from Springfield back to Urbana ($150), where Twin City Doozie confirmed that the engine would have to be overhauled.

We have since meticulously investigated the possible causes for this incident. There was no oil *leak*. The Doozie was always parked in one of two places—our driveway at home and my parking place at the University of Illinois. There is no oil in our driveway, and none at my parking spot at the U of I.

My first inclination was to blame Twin City Doozie. They have serviced our car—they have been the *only* ones who have serviced it.

Then we talked to friends with the same model Doozie. Most had had to have their valve guides replaced. We had not. *All* believed that faulty valve guides might have caused excessive use of oil.

We also talked to independent mechanics who assured us that no car with only 10,000 miles on it should use 4 quarts of oil in 4,000 miles.

A recent conversation with a fellow-Doozie owner resulted in his checking his Doozie. Dip-stick showed less than 1/2-quart of oil in his car. His oil light had never come on either. But he was able to save his Doozie as a result of our conversation.

As you can tell, I am terribly upset by these experiences. We obviously cannot afford to spend $1400 on a car with only 14,000 miles on it. Neither can we, as folks of only modest means, afford to junk it and buy another car.

Can you give us any help? We chose the Doozie in the first place because of its fine reputation and because we believed Japanese work-ethics assured us of a fine-quality car. Obviously, we have been sorely disappointed. It will have cost us over $243 a month to run this car (not including routine maintenance, gas, and oil), if we have to bear this expense ourselves. Hardly an "economy" car. And hardly a car you would recommend to your friends. Frankly, at this point, there is just no way we can come up with $1400 for repairs which we feel are in no way our fault. Our dream of an "economy" car has turned into a nightmare of excessive expenses.

I believe that we deserve some kind of recompense for these expenses and inconveniences. And, having heard of your genuine interest in maintaining good customer relations here in the States, I hope you agree.

May we hear from you soon?

Louise W. Steele
(Mrs. James C.)

cc: Manager, Twin-City Doozie

V.I.N. SBC-6133419
Engine No. EB3-1056949

FIVE

1   Like J. D. Salinger's "The Catcher in the Rye" and
Joseph Heller's "Catch-22," John Irving's "The World
According to Garp," published in 1978, was a novel
that spoke to the sensibility of its time and in particular to the sensibility of youth.

2   Partly, it was the book's exuberant inventiveness
that explained its appeal. Mr. Irving's near-epic tale of
the birth, life and death of his writer hero, T. S. Garp,
was packed with an array of extravagant incidents and
bizarre, emphatically contemporary characters: radical
feminists, transsexuals, rapists, mad terrorists, prep-
pies and jocks. Partly, too, it was the way the novel
mixed outrageous comedy and stomach-turning hor-
ror, conveying a sense of the world as a crazy and
dangerous place, constantly threatened by the Undertoad—Garp's son's mishearing of a warning to
"beware the undertow"—and the conceit used by the
author to illustrate life's pointless tragedies and ran-

dom violence. But what made "Garp" so special was the affirmation, despite the pain it dramatized, of the redeeming power of compassion and love—its tenderness.

3   Since it's precisely this tenderness that the current adaptation of "The World According to Garp" most fully captures, many fans of the book will also be fans of the movie. Besides, as directed by George Roy Hill from a witty and brilliantly compressed screenplay by Steve Tesich, the film brings to the screen more of Garp's dizzyingly eventful story than anyone might have thought possible.

4   A chronological series of brief, often richly resonant sequences depicting phases of the hero's life shapes the movie. We first see Garp as the adored, gurgling infant of his resolutely unmarried mother, Nurse Jenny Fields (very well played by Glenn Close), then watch him as a young boy at Jenny's knee, drawing imaginary pictures of the dead flyer who fathered him. Later scenes show him as an adolescent at a New England prep school (it's here that Robin Williams takes over the role), as the happy, then cuckolded, husband of his childhood sweetheart, Helen (Mary Beth Hurt), and as the delighted and then bereaved parent, sitting at the edge of the sea, thinking of the child he's lost and of the Undertoad.

5   This moment and others focusing on Garp as wistful son and caring father, rather than on Garp as writer, give the film its immense store of feeling. Similarly charged are the many sequences treating Nurse Jenny, feminist leader and beloved mentor of 6'4" transsexual Roberta Muldoon (John Lithgow, who deserves every award in sight for his superb performance), and the fanatical Ellen Jamesians, who have cut out their

tongues to protest the rape and similar disfigurement of a young girl.

6   Indeed, the film's treatment of weird types such as these may be its most striking accomplishment. The challenge of bringing "Garp" to the screen didn't lie simply in the novel's incredible fullness or even its un-cinematic subject—the development of a writer. It was that so many of the characters were grotesques who might have seemed even more so on screen. But direc-tor Hill has managed to make these misfits soft and human and, more startling still, less pitiful than ad-mirable in their courage to be different. Mr. Hill has also managed to treat tastefully—mostly by leaving off-screen—some of the book's strongest and most unsettling materials: for example, the circumstances of Garp's conception and the macabre accident that costs one of Garp's sons an eye, another his life, and also un-mans his wife's lover.

7   The novel's devotees will probably bemoan the loss of such stuff, since it was the difficult-to-take passages that gave the novel its compelling blackness. This blackness is pretty much missing from the film. It's also true that the film lacks much of the novel's energy and style. Still, director Hill has eschewed the post-card prettiness he showed in movies like "The Sting" and "The Great Waldo Pepper." What's bothersome is that he hasn't really settled on anything distinctive to take its place, ending up with a movie that, considering its content, often looks bland. Of course, one can also take issue with the casting of Robin Williams, who has neither the appeal nor the range to make quite enough of his role, though it's true that Garp functions largely as an observer on the one hand and a creative con-sciousness on the other, and just may be the least in-teresting character in his world.

8   Certainly, these limitations are considerable, yet to stress them seems carping in light of this immensely intelligent and intensely tolerant film's achievements. There are moments that are remarkably authentic—many having to do with the children the film not only loves but has sharply observed. And several sequences are truly inspired: the credit sequence, for instance, in which we watch baby Garp, his expressions continually changing as he bounces in and out of the frame; or a scene taking us inside Garp's imagination, as he builds from a fragment of conversation overheard, a pair of dropped gloves and the sight of a piano being hoisted in the air, his first and "saddest story."

9   Above all, there's the sense of the richness and ongoing quality of existence that the film so fully conveys. "Garp" makes graphic what Jenny Fields is after when she instructs her son: "Everybody dies. The thing is to have a life before you do."—Joy Gould Boyum, "A Striking Spin Through Garp's Weird World"

SIX

1   Man has built two basic kinds of control into his machines. One, known as "open-loop control," makes it possible for a machine, once started, to proceed as if by clockwork through a pre-established pattern of performance. The other, called "closed-loop control," or, more familiarly, "feedback," makes it possible for a machine to check, correct and control its own operations while they are in progress.

2   Neither type of control is new to the age of electronics. Hero of Alexandria, some 2,000 years back, created a simple, cause-and-effect, open-loop control

when he devised a linkage of expanding hot air, water, bucket, spindles and counterweight, that swung open the doors of a temple when a priest lighted a fire on a nearby altar. In the 18th Century, James Watt used a classic feedback control to maintain the desired speed of his steam engine. Metal balls were mounted on a revolving shaft geared to the engine's main output shaft. When speed began building up, centrifugal force caused the spinning balls to lift upward and outward, like airplane swings on a carnival ride. As they did so, they partially closed the throttle, thus reducing the speed of the engine. A drop in speed below the desired level produced the reverse effect.

3   Open-loop controls abound in today's machines—in the start-to-stop performance of an automatic washing machine, an automatic record changer, a coffee-vending machine. But the heart and soul of full automation, of the most advanced stage of the man-machine relationship, is the dynamic, self-correcting, self-regulating dominion of feedback.

4   Feedback devices maintain desired standards of machine performance by generating what control engineers call the "error signal"—in effect, supplying answers to the machine's question, "How am I doing?" An example may be seen in the simple thermostatic furnace control. A thermostat is set at 72°F. If the room temperature drops below that, the thermostatic sensor feeds back an error signal; the thermostat kicks on the furnace; the temperature rises to the desired level, and the thermostat shuts off the furnace. The relationship of furnace to room temperature to thermostat and back to furnace is direct, interacting, closed, as in a chain or loop—hence the term closed-loop control.

5   Although feedback control devices were known two centuries ago, they began to come into their own in the 1920s. This breakthrough was neither isolated nor overnight. It could not have happened without the vacuum tube to amplify and relay the sensors' feeble signals. It could not have happened without advances in the sensors themselves—without transducers for sensing pressures, temperatures, forces, velocities, volumes of light and sound; without detectors for spotting overheat, overload, moisture, flow—all the clever, bioelectronic devices that enable a machine to hear and see, touch and feel. Nor would the breakthrough have taken place so long before anyone really expected it without the technological thrust of World War II, that evolved brilliant uses of feedback in automatic detection, in tracking and firing systems of al kinds, and, above all, in the proximity fuze, whose radar feedback exploded its shell the instant it came within a set distance of its target.

6   Today feedback is at work on every hand, automating processes that are vital to our health and comfort as well as to the nation's economy. It regulates the flow of electricity in our power lines, maintains the quality of our oil and gasoline, our steel, copper and concrete, and ensures the consistency of many foods and drugs. It has had particular impact on the sprawling, 156-billion-dollar-a-year metalworking industry, because it has made possible self-regulating automatic control—called "numerical control" by the industry—of machine-tool operations.—Robert O'Brien, *Machines*

A FEW EXERCISES
IN STYLE

These exercises are designed to illustrate the ideas in Chapter Six, on the sentence. But they will be most helpful if you have read the other chapters too.

To write a sentence well, you must keep in mind your argument, your audience, and the words you use. You should also ask how well the sentence explains your ideas, and how it fits into the sentences before and after it (which implies *organization*). A sentence is more than syntax.

In fact, you can cure many a sick sentence by crossing it out, and talking to your reader ("Here is what I want you to think about this...."), and then writing the sentence on paper as clearly as you can.

Look back at the second paragraph on this page: "To write a sentence well ...." In my first draft, I tried to get my material into this sentence:

Many a bad sentence is bad because ....

I stopped because I could not phrase the reason that had to come after *because*. I tried this:

Many a sentence is bad for reasons other than syntax.

Not good enough either. Syntax is not a "reason." Also, I had tried to jam too many abstract ideas into a short space—ideas about *sentence, badness, reason, syntax.*

Starting the sentence again, I expanded it into a paragraph of three sentences, the last one acting rather like a punch line:

A sentence is more than syntax.

In the rewriting you have just seen, many elements of the writing process got involved—handling of ideas, arrangement of sentence parts, the musical cadence of the phrases, the noise of the words themselves. Note the *s* alliteration:

A *S*entence is more than *S*yntax.

And feel the beat of the line:

A SENtence is MORE than SYNtax.

Like poetry, prose has rhythm, although the rhythm is usually different. Only a computer, or possibly a bureaucrat, could write rhythmless prose.

Now we will inspect a few bad sentences and rewrite them for clarity, force, and rhythm. We should agree from the start that to rewrite is automatically to change meaning. Authorities in linguistics tell us that different *forms* supply different meanings. Change anything, even a single word, and you change meaning. Furthermore, and more to our point here, we are trying to think more clearly by writing more clearly—to make clear writing and thinking habitual.

BAD SENTENCE: The loss of professors' credibility represents an indispensable foundation upon which authority structures are undermined.

Why is the sentence bad?

1. It is vague and fuzzy.
2. It has too many abstract ideas.
3. It is noun-y. A sure sign of badness is one abstract noun modifying another: *authority structures.*
4. It is illogical. It says that a *loss represents* a *foundation.*

Always inspect a sentence for what it tries to tell the reader. Usually, in skeleton form, this amounts to:

Who does what   *or*   What does what

Who is what   *or*   What is what

Technique for rewrite:
   Simplify the wording. Try *who does what.* Break up the sentence into units *(keep on chunking).* Change the abstract subject of the main clause into a specific word. The sentence implies cause and effect. Therefore we can build this into our rewrite:

In the past 20 years, the college professor has lost his credibility. Students no longer automatically believe what he tells them. As a result, . . .

Twice now, you have seen me expand a sentence to make it more readable. Fairly often nowadays, sentences are so compressed you cannot tell what they mean:

Such an industry is typically risk-aversive.

Reading that is like trying to bite into a football; your teeth bounce off it.

If a sentence needs compression, compress it:

NOT SO GOOD: Prose, like poetry, is metrical, which simply means that it has rhythmic sounds, although they usually form a different kind of rhythm. (my first version: 22 words)

BETTER: Like poetry, prose has rhythm, although the rhythm is usually different. (my second version: 11 words)

Here is the first line of a will:

BAD SENTENCE: I, Jane Doe, being of sound and disposing mind and memory, and not acting under duress or the undue influence of any person whatsoever, do hereby make, publish, and declare this to be my last will and testament. (38 words)

Of this sentence, David Mellinkoff (Professor of Law at UCLA) says: "It has the sound of law; that's all. Despite its detractors, the law is more than tinkle. The only legal substance in the form that counts in the will can be said better in four words: *This is my will.*" (4 words)

Here are a few bad sentences to practice on. Typical rewrites are shown on pp. 127–29.

1. The St. Louis Eagles' best receiver was outstanding this year and was able to move fast and deceptively on most occasions when he wasn't injured.

2. The Republicrat position on the slums is a philosophy of understanding concerning the poor found in ghetto areas in terms of a clarification of the problems to be solved.

3. The best modern writers choose clear sentence patterns by a process which is difficult to explain using the ideas in standard grammar.

4. Parental endeavors in regard to education suggest an ambitious drive toward self-improvement and an interest in upward mobility.

5. My work helped me in respect to a wide variety of people and also to share my ideas with others.

6. The conclusion of this writer in the final analysis is that the basic question of the controversy is on who or what authority should the sale of marijuana be allowed.

7. My research is valuable in regard to the information gained concerning the opinions of students on coed living in the dormitories and because it did not cost much to get the material.

8. It requires extreme patience in order to still have cheerfulness at the end of a day of hard work dealing with customer complaints.

9. The tree pruner's plan for cutting a tree is a result of skills learned over years of training and experience.

10. After explaining my job to me, there was a vehicle sent by the Head Ranger to take me to the office.

11. There have been several proposals which have since come forth about what to do with the dangerous crossing south of Fresno.

12. Last year the campus had a great increase in narcotics arrests, most of them on a drug possession charge or for using drugs.

13. The next point to make about idiom differences explains one of the most difficult problems for foreign speakers of English.

14. It must be considered a possibility that the student nurse must be able to face physical damage, broken bones, cranial disorders, pregnancy, or even death.

15. Here is a typical opener for a contract. In its own way, it serves the practical legal purpose of identifying the contract—naming the parties, and giving the date and place of making.

   THIS AGREEMENT, made and entered into this 10th day of January, 1981, in the City of Los Angeles, State of California, by and between John Doak, hereinafter sometimes referred to as and called the Party of the First Part, and the Plotz Corporation, a corporation duly organized and existing under and by virtue of the laws of the State of Delaware, hereinafter sometimes referred to as and called the Party of the Second Part,

   WITNESSETH . . . .—David Mellinkoff, *Legal Writing: Sense and Nonsense*

SUGGESTED FORMS FOR YOUR BUSINESS ESSAY OR MESSAGE

As you can tell from my comments elsewhere in this book, I don't care much for "canned" pieces of writing. The older textbooks used to give a special form for every message—and the messages were endlessly classified and subclassified. (Some recent textbooks still do this.)

Yet the prescribed forms sometimes don't fit your essay or message very well. And readers tend to get bored or downright rebellious when they see the same dull form come chugging around the corner. But—and there is always a *but* in such matters—you should know the form before deciding to deviate from it. And of course the standard form is on occasion exactly what you need.

So . . .

MEMO

```
                                        DATE:

      TO:

      FROM:

      SUBJECT:

      _____

      _____

      _____  MESSAGE  _____

      _____

      _____

      _____

      _____
```

PROPOSAL

A proposal is your *solution* to a *problem.*

Introduction   State the problem clearly and specifically.

Body   Give your solution.
- Describe your requirements in people, material, or equipment.
- Give the costs involved.
- Give a schedule for completing the work.
- Add any illustrations—tables, figures, graphs—that will help the reader.

Conclude   Restate your solution or recommendation.

BUSINESS LETTER

```
                                    1001 Calhoun Avenue
                                    Columbus, Ohio   43215
                                    June 23, 1983


        Mr. Weston Sharpe
        Customer Services
        Imperial Manufacturing Company
        4207 Disston Avenue
        Westville, Kentucky   40881

        Subject:  (optional)

        Dear Mr. Sharpe:


        _____

        _____

        _____

        _____

                        (MESSAGE)

        _____

        _____

        _____


        _____

        _____

        _____

        _____

        _____

                                    Sincerely yours,

                                    Ms. Verdeen Smith
```

REPORT

Here is the full form. Cut anything you think is unnecessary.

Title page.

Letter of transmittal. Explain (a) why the report was written, (b) what special problems you faced, and (c) whether future work on the problem may be necessary.

Table of contents.

Summary (or *abstract*). A brief synopsis of the report.

Introduction. Give pertinent information concerning the subject or the report: "background material," definitions of terms, special explanation of procedures.

Body. Give all the evidence, facts, data.

Conclusions. Briefly draw together your explanation of the material in the body. Answer the question: "What does all this add up to?"

Recommendations. (Can be combined with the previous section.) Answer the question: "What should be done about the problem or project?"

Footnotes and bibliography. Only if required.

Appendix. Contains what might not fit easily into other sections; for example, maps, diagrams, graphs, photographs, charts, work sheets, questionnaires, specifications, etc.).

BAD-NEWS MESSAGE

As the name implies, the bad-news message is one that the receiver does not want to get. He prefers not to read it; he may be greatly disappointed or even enraged when he reads it. For in it you are telling the reader that he won't get the job, the loan, the application for gas heat approved, the delivery of a new car on time. A certain delicacy is required here.

- Consider using a *buffer:*
  "We have carefully read your application, and are impressed by your qualifications. . . . However, . . . "
  "Your proposal for a new water system has many obvious merits, among them . . . . Yet, . . ."
  "I have talked with all members of the committee about your situation, but . . . ."
- Make your negative statement *early;* don't make the reader wait and wonder.
- Make your negative statement *clear;* ambiguity irritates.
- Be factual; if possible, say *why* your news is bad.
- If you can, leave hope for the future—all is not lost!
- Use a friendly (but not flippant) tone throughout.

RÉSUMÉ

Consider the résumé as a brief message that *sells* you (and your skills) to the reader.

- - - - - - *Your name* - - - - - -
- Job wanted (if relevant, state your preferred geographical location)
- Qualifications for the job
- Education
- Experience
- Activities, interests, honors
- References

NOTE: I could give much more information on the résumé—write a chapter on how you might write one. There are many variables: How experienced are you?

What kind of job do you want? What kind of reader(s) are you aiming for? If you are a new college graduate, consider doing a one-page résumé. If you are experienced, consider making it longer. In either case, you may want to attach a cover letter.

Above all, use common sense. Put yourself in the reader's place. After reading your résumé, would *you* want to hire you?

REWRITES OF BAD SENTENCES (pp. 119–21)

NOTE: Consider a rewrite as a stylistic "finger exercise." Limber up the writing fingers and awaken the brain. Try different attitudes and viewpoints. For number 2, we might scribble such sentences as these:

—What does the typical Republicrat believe can be done in the slums? Answer: Understand the poor, and you solve their problems.

—We Republicrats believe this about the ghetto: Before you can solve its problems, you must understand them.

—The Republicrats believe that the key to slum problems is understanding them.

—Problems in the ghetto, say the Republicrats, cannot be solved until they are understood. [What does *they* refer to?]

—Those Republicrats who live in the ghetto want their problems understood and solved.

—As a Republicrat, my philosophy concerning slum living is that . . . . [I give up on this one!]

—In the slums, people have problems. Senate Republicrats are determined to analyze and solve those problems. [Does that sound like a lead in the six o'clock news?]

—Etc.

1. On most occasions, when he wasn't injured, the St. Louis Eagles' best receiver was outstanding this year—able to move fast and deceptively.

2. See NOTE above.

3. The best modern writers choose sentence patterns by a mental process of some kind. But standard grammar does not explain that process very well.

4. Why do many parents push their children so hard in school? One reason may be selfish—for their children they want the success they did not have.

5. In my work I learned two things: to get along with a variety of people and to share my ideas with them.

6. Finally, here is the basic question. Who has the authority to allow the sale of marijuana?

7. Because my research collected student opinions on coed living in the dormitories, it is valuable. [Omit the irrelevant stuff on *cost*?]

8. At the end of a hard day of dealing with customer complaints, you don't feel very cheerful.

9. Before cutting a tree, the experienced pruner makes a careful plan.

10. After explaining my job, the Head Ranger sent me to the office in a car.

11. The County Board has made several proposals for improving the dangerous crossing south of Fresno.

12. Last year, campus police arrested more students on drug charges.

13. Foreigners find English idioms very difficult to learn.

14. As a student nurse, be prepared for anything—from simple broken bones to patients who die unexpectedly after you have given them tender care for weeks.

15.   AGREEMENT, made 10th January, 1981, in Los Angeles, California, between John Doak, and Plotz Corporation, of Delaware.—as rewritten by David Mellinkoff, prof. of law

INDEX